Striped Bass Fishing

STRIPED BASS FISHING

Frank Woolner
and Henry Lyman

Lyons & Burford, Publishers

THE SALTWATER SPORTSMAN LIBRARY

PRINTED IN THE UNITED STATES OF AMERICA
10 9 8 7 6 5 4

Library of Congress Cataloging in Publication Data

Woolner, Frank, 1916–
  Striped bass fishing.

  Rev. ed. of: The complete book of striped bass
fishing/Henry Lyman, Frank Woolner. 1954.
    "A Nick Lyons book."
    Includes index.
    1. Striped bass fishing.   I. Lyman, Henry, 1915–
II. Lyman, Henry, 1915–   . Complete book of striped
bass fishing.   III. Title.
SH351.B3W66   1983   799.1'758   82–20300
ISBN 0-8329-0279-9
ISBN 0-8329-0281-1 (paperback)

Contents

Acknowledgments

To ACKNOWLEDGE THE HELP OF ALL WHO HAVE MADE this book possible is itself an impossible task. Their name is legion and, to be truthful, many names were never known. A little scrap of information given by an Outer Banker on a wintry beach at Hatteras, the laconic observation from a canny mate aboard a charter boat off Sandy Hook, each was filed away in our memories, to be pieced together later as a possible theory or technique developed. Names are also buried in the mass of correspondence that has accumulated over the years. We only hope that our helpers will read these words and take credit where credit is due.

We fish during every moment we can sneak away from the office and now, with more leisure time on our hands, we hope to sneak away more often. However, neither of us can hope to cover every hot spot, every method used, every detail of bass fishing. We have therefore depended to a large extent upon numerous other anglers, qualified colleagues in the business of outdoor writing, and authoritative marine biologists whose questions, and balanced answers, have helped to solve some problems of our own.

The source of many tips, techniques, and even demonstrations of success is the hard-fishing group, past and present, that has acted in the capacity of a field staff for *Salt Water Sportsman Magazine*. Anglers all, these specialists have unselfishly documented tricks and methods peculiar to the particular areas where they are stationed. They will recognize personal contributions and, we trust, will accept our thanks as they read.

Among the scientists, those of the National Marine Fisheries Service and many researchers working at the state level on striped bass are owed particular thanks. We have picked their brains with the result that their findings have been incorporated into our text. Two names should be noted for their early work in this field—Dr. Daniel Merriman, retired Yale professor, whose paper on the striper published in 1941 established the fact that the fish do indeed migrate; and Dr. Edward C. Raney, a professor at Cornell, who pulled together all known information on the species in a masterful summary printed in 1952.

At the organizational and, for want of a better term, political levels, we are indebted to such groups as the Atlantic States Marine Fisheries Commission, which is now in the process of implementing a striped bass fishery management plan along the eastern seaboard. United States Senator John H. Chafee of Rhode Island should be given special credit for supporting funding of $4.7 million at the federal level for striper research to determine causes for decline in bass populations. The three-year project, initiated in 1979, has resulted in a mass of published material which has been grist to our mill.

The late Dr. John H. Cunningham of Brookline and Wareham, Massachusetts, kindly supplied us with valuable records of the old bassing clubs in New England, as well as the early history of bass fishing elsewhere. These records are now in the archives of the International Game Fish Association in Fort Lauderdale, Florida, for the use of any who might be interested in pursuing history further.

Photographs throughout the book, unless otherwise credited, were taken from the archives of *Salt Water Sportsman* and we are indebted to the staff of that magazine for permission to use them.

Finally, we thank countless numbers of newcomers on today's far-flung striper coasts—young men and women whose questions and observations dating back to the 1930s have sent us scurrying to our files, written and unwritten, and have made it necessary for us to conduct on-site research out where the world's oceans pose their magnificent challenge. In this book, we deal with the past and present of striped bass fishing, fully aware of the fact that today's fledglings will be tomorrow's consummate authorities.

Introduction

ANY WORK DEDICATED TO STRIPED BASS FISHING IS, by nature and content, unlike any other volume under the sun. For that reason, we feel morally obliged to launch this craft with a wry warning rather than with a bottle of champagne.

After all, you asked for it. Every one of you wants to get into striped bass fishing and learn the secrets of this highly popular sport as it is practiced on the Atlantic and Pacific Coasts, in fresh water impoundments where stocking has proved successful—wherever the pugnacious linesided warrior roams. Certainly everyone wants to know more about modern tackle and strategy on site. Finally, everyone wants to catch a bass.

That is why *The Complete Book of Striped Bass Fishing* was first written and published in 1954. Meanwhile, the world spins and times change subtly. Old anglers surely get no younger, and there has been steady progress in the knowledge painfully gathered by erudite scientists and innovative fishermen, who have built new tactics and techniques on the solid foundation provided by their elders.

This volume—though it is now more modestly titled *Striped Bass Fishing*—might be called "the same old lady with a pretty new face." It has been thoroughly re-written and updated as a timely examination of striped bass and bass fishing in the 1980s. No segment of history has been deleted, no ancient trick of the trade ignored. However, a great deal has happened during close to 30 years of steady advancement in angling techniques, in tackle, and in basic knowledge of the fish itself.

Marine biology, particularly as it applies to the well-being of the striped bass, has progressed very rapidly since the early 1950s. Interdependence among the various species that swim along with the striper is receiving more and more attention among scientists. We know more now than we did in our salad days, yet we remain puzzled by a multitude of contradictory theories. While a few far-out ideas are worth pursuing, there has always been a tendency among certain honest types, who may lack scholarly training, to lash out at the cautious findings of professionals. Too many of the new messiahs lack proof, rely on shot-in-the-dark hypotheses, and are prone to push panic buttons. In spite of all they have not caught a single fish—there must be some reason for this lack of success. We wish them well, but note ruefully that a surprising percentage of the know-all folks have never studied history. That is a major sin, for history has a habit of repeating itself.

This book, therefore, examines advances in hard knowledge about the fish and the state of the fishery. As a striper buff, you are not going to find many radical departures here or any pat solutions to age-old problems. Our authority continues to be the highly educated professional. He may sometimes be wrong, but he is more likely to be right than the everyday angler who has decided to become an expert *sans* training, without a sophisticated laboratory at his disposal and without the computerized space-age instruments so important to in-depth research. Such "experts" are, unhappily, always ready to make hay with political rabble-rousers, who themselves have personal axes to grind.

This book contains an updating of all techniques germane to practical sport fishing for striped bass. There are new sections dealing with methods that have evolved during the past 30 years, containing evaluation of the current and much-advanced tackle, and detailing the development of sophisticated boats and various electronic aids now widely employed by suntanned regulars on all coasts. Times have changed since 1954 and no doubt will be changed again 30 years hence. We simply have tried to halt the pendulum to note what is going on right now.

One thing never changes. Striped bass fishing is arguably the toughest, most muscle-busting game ever camouflaged by the name *angling*. You will walk miles and cast for hours, clamber over perilous, barnacle-encrusted boulders, and get dumped on your beam ends by combers that seem to come out of nowhere. You will be wet and have sand in your ears; you will fish day and night, from the beaches, from rocky jetties, from the pitching, slippery decks of specialized boats. Inevitably you will spend more money than prudence allows on items ranging from four-wheel-drive beach buggies to electronic fishfinders. You will seek, always and forever, for a thing called "blitz," which is as elusive as pirate's gold.

In your search, most of the regulars will be very pleasant while they tell you absolutely nothing about the current hot spots. The best gimmick is to join a local salt water fishing club, make friends among the squint-eyed members, and get invited to join them on a sortie. Ten to one, even if this wonderful invitation is extended, you will be sworn to secrecy about the location of good grounds and the right tides, times, and winds. Best keep your mouth shut and learn.

Inevitably, the sport becomes an obsession. By comparison, flounder hunters are well-mannered Saturday-afternoon enthusiasts. Tuna fishermen and billfish buffs go out with the dawn and return at sunset. Even those wild-eyed characters who worship at the shrine of tarpon, bluefish, yellowtail, or albacore manage to see their wives and children on occasion. Not so the salty basser.

That worthy centurion rarely thinks of his conjugal barracks during an optimum fishing season. His begrudged non-fishing hours are filled with the rigging of plugs and tin squids, spoons, lead-head jigs, and feathers. His refrigerator bulges with rigged eels and eels yet to be rigged, with crawly sea worms tenderly bedded in weed. The true addict is attuned to tides and wind directions, moon phases and barometric changes. At every opportunity, he goes—and he stays. If his wife is smart, she sues for divorce on grounds of desertion, or goes fishing too.

Once committed to this strangely narcotic affliction, there is no known cure or escape. So, if you are not ready to consign your soul to the sea, sand, and stripers, do not buy this book and do not read it. If some fiendish friend gives you a copy, burn it immediately.

Let us assume, however, that you are too far gone for redemption. You have tasted the wind-whipped brine, felt the elemental fury of high surf crashing against scalloped dunes, the surge and flow of river currents, the spectacular power of offshore rips. Perhaps you have seen a huge bass slice through the heart of an emerald comber and have taken the fish, or lost it. The end result is the same.

In that case, like the authors of this book and like all the fevered fanatics of the striper coast, you *know* that this is a game without parallel, a sport compounded of many things: of skill and hard work, of exultation in battling the elements, of outwitting and catching a wonderfully unpredictable warrior. You are a striped bass nut and there is no turning back!

This is your book. In it we endeavor to tell the story of modern striped bass fishing: the hows, the whys, and the wherefores of tackle, live baits, artificial lures, and strategy throughout the striper's range. If it is possible for us to help you catch even one grand fish in the surf or from an offshore rip, a sod bank, an inlet, or tidal river, our aim will be realized. There is, however, one chapter we cannot write, one that is yours alone to create in your own way.

That chapter, of course, is personal and will be based on a sense of the magnificence and the mystery of the striper coast itself, the clean, clear air, the sunlight sparkling on miles of foaming, tumbling waves. We are not masters enough to transmit to you the haunted and prescient feeling when you cast lure or bait into the hissing brine on a running tide in that pale hour before dawn, or the excitement you experience in a howling gale, riding a plunging bass boat through the stinging spray of an offshore rip while sea birds wheel and cry.

A bass fisherman lives for these things, and so many more: The wild beauty of a beach that could, for all the evidence at hand, be a forgotten frontier with sanderlings quick-stepping in the wash. The ever-changing ocean, silk-smooth and calm or raging under a demonic wind; the pulsing tides; phosphorescence under a midnight sky, sparkling like a billion diamonds under boots or keel. Finally, a God-granted hour when stripers forget that they are hard to catch and come rocketing up to smash at every lure thrown their way.

Records are made to be broken. Every striped bass fisherman is convinced that some time, at some magic hour of dawn or midday or deep night, he or she will personally hang a fish to make the great ones of the past blush with shame. For an enthusiast, no striped monster is too ridiculous for belief, no angling triumph beyond possibility. If we can set your feet on the salt-washed path to such success, we rest content.

1 · Early History

RED-EYED AND WEARY, WITH A STUBBLE OF BEARD ON his sunburned face, the striped bass fisherman hunches over a cup of coffee. Although he has fished around the clock without success, he believes sincerely and a little madly that they *must* hit on the next turn of the tide. Hope persists and, when the moon exerts its mysterious pull on the ocean waters again, he will be back at the sea's edge, drawn by a force equally powerful and perhaps even more mysterious.

To pinpoint reasons for the tremendous appeal of striped bass angling is nearly impossible. There are other fish that grow bigger, fight harder, and are more difficult to catch, yet the striper has a fanatical human following that compares to none. No single species has changed the habits of the coastal angler more than this rugged, fascinating, unpredictable prima donna of the sea.

Men of absolute integrity in other matters have been known to cheat and lie when taxed with questions concerning their striper fishing. There is one case on modern record of a surf fishermen losing his mind over the sport. He was found by his companions rigidly standing near the surf muttering, "Just one more cast!" Family tensions may reach a breaking point as the head of the house vanishes, night after night, to pit his wits against a comparatively unintelligent fish. Despite these effects on humans, the bassing fraternity continues to hold its chosen species as a fish apart from the more ordinary salt water angling targets.

Perhaps the characteristics of the bass itself are a major factor in its popularity. Since colonial times, the striper's appearance, fighting qualities, and tastiness have been sources of admiration.

"The bass is one of the best fishes in the country," William Wood wrote in 1634, "and although men are soon wearied with other fish, yet are they never with bass. It is a delicate, fine, fat, fast fish having a bone in its head which contains a saucerful of marrow sweet and good, pleasant to the pallat and wholesome to the stomach." Whether the marrow to which Wood referred are the brains or cheeks of the striper, we cannot say, but his observations are as sound today as they were when tackle consisted of a cod line and a hook baited with lobster tail.

The importance of the striped bass in colonial times was based on the species' value as a source of food, not as a sporting proposition. Indeed fragile old records indicate that our grim Pilgrim Fathers defined sport as unholy frivolity, so it is likely that Cotton Mather would have sent any dedicated and unrepentent angler to the gibbet, just as he arranged the hanging of nineteen so-called "witches" in Salem. Sport, for the sweet sake of sport alone, prospered well after Mather in his long black gown presumably answered to celestial judges far sterner than he.

Aside from the sometimes illicit joy of hauling fishes out of the sea, American angling for striped bass developed slowly, hardly recognized as a game men like to play until the 1800s. Even at the turn of that century "tackle" invariably consisted of hand lines, hooks, sinkers, and natural baits. Heavy drails were used by skilled practitioners in a method called heave-and-haul. This consisted of coiling an adequate yardage of line on the beach, after which the drail was whirled about the caster's head and heaved far out from shore. It was an operation that required split-second timing and work-toughened fists to maintain the hand-over-hand retrieve alone, not to mention fighting large bass.

Stripers have finned through American history from the very beginning. To connect them with railroad mergers, textile mills, and million-dollar

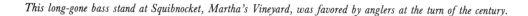

This long-gone bass stand at Squibnocket, Martha's Vineyard, was favored by anglers at the turn of the century.

combines may seem peculiar, yet this great ocean sport fish played an important role in clinching some of the largest business deals in the United States.

Shortly after the Civil War had run its bloody course, bass clubs, organized by some of the most prominent industrialists, statesmen, and businessmen of the day, came into being. Members settled the affairs of the growing country after the day's catch had been weighed and a cheering glass poured.

Although most of these tycoons had their main offices in New York City, their fishing grounds for the most part were in the vicinity of the Elizabeth Island chain off the coast of Massachusetts and on a few selected islands off Rhode Island. With the exception of the Providence Club, which was composed of Rhode Islanders, few New England names can be found in the old membership lists of such organizations as the Cuttyhunk Club, Squibnocket Club, or clubs established at Pasque Island, West Island and Cohasset Narrows. Evidently, for New England summer residents, Cape Cod, Martha's Vineyard, Nantucket and Block Island provided all the striper fishing they needed, and on an informal basis.

A look at the ledgers of these old clubs, kept meticulously in a fine copperplate hand, reveals some interesting points. Wine and liquor expenses often equalled, or even exceeded, the charges for food. And the food was substantial. Genio C. Scott in his classic *Fishing in American Waters*, published in 1875, mentions a West Island breakfast of "tea and coffee, with broiled bluefish, striped bass and scopogue, or with broiled chicken and beefsteak." After a day with the bass, the "sports" settled in for serious eating and drinking. Three stars and a rocking chair on a blue field formed the flag of the Cuttyhunk Club before bourbon had displaced brandy as a popular potion in the Northeast.

Pigeons, pigeon feed, and pigeon care were charged against the club as a whole rather than against the account of an individual. These birds were not to provide the members with a pigeon shoot, a favorite sport of the time: They were for communications. Since a catboat or yawl, sailed from the mainland, supplied the only regular human contact with the outside world, carrier pigeons were a necessity for men of affairs who had dealings in the distant city of New York. Elihu Root, one of the prominent members of the Squibnocket Club, would have been as helpless without his winged messengers as a modern statesman would be without a telephone.

Only in the West Island Club, which was located near the cities of Fairhaven and New Bedford, was modern communication available. One of the first Morse telegraph offices ran a branch line, paid for by the members, to that island. According to the records, the volume of traffic sent from the club overwhelmed the local operator to such an extent that he demanded—and got—an assistant.

Communications were not limited to affairs of business and state, however. These men liked bass fishing and they did their best to keep in touch with their quarry. Bait therefore loomed large on the budget. A single lobster tail on an angler's hook cost little, but the hundreds of pounds of ground menhaden, crab, lobster, and eel used as chum totalled high. Bass caught and not used by the members were sold in the market and the money received from the sale was applied against the bait bill. Rarely did this account get in the black.

Once the clubhouse had been built, upkeep was not high. These comfortable "camps" were the centers for social and business activities. The clubhouses, however, were not the important structures as far as the fishermen were concerned. Bass stands were.

Stands for the most part were made by driving steel rods into the rocks to support narrow wooden walkways. At the end of each walkway was a small platform from which the angler cast. Waves often broke over these platforms to the discomfort of the fisherman and his gaffer, who was stationed on the rocks below. During the winter months, when storms lashed the islands, it was customary to take up the structural planks and store them until the start of the next season.

The chummer, who was an important assistant to the angler, might double as a gaffer also. Usually, however, chum was distributed from a small boat stationed a short distance offshore and upcurrent to toll the fish to the stand. The slick might be increased by an additional chummer on the rocks below the stand or by ground fish tossed from the platform itself. The basic technique of chumming still produces stripers today.

The old stand supports have now rusted away, yet the angling antiquarian can find their locations easily enough by spotting the drilled rocks at low tide. These locations, despite years of coastal erosion, are still good bassing areas. In the 1950s, a property owner at Squibnocket re-installed one of the stands at its former location, caught bass from it, but abandoned the project later because of the costs involved in repairs and maintenance.

Most famous of the old bassing clubs were those built at Cuttyhunk and Pasque Islands; on Squibnocket Point at the southeastern tip of Martha's Vineyard, where both the Squibnocket and Providence clubs were located; on West Island; and at Cohasset Narrows near the present town of Buzzards Bay. At the turn of the century, Nature stepped in to hasten abandonment of these angling organizations. Striped bass all but vanished from the New England coast during the early 1900s and the gatherings of wealthy, talented, rugged anglers, who fished with knuckle-buster reels as the waves broke over their heads, vanished with them. Only on Pasque and Cuttyhunk Islands do the old clubhouses, now converted to residential use, still stand as evidence of a past era.

After the golden age of bass, brandy, and pigeons, the fishery virtually collapsed as far as anglers were concerned. However, a turning point in the

The Cuttyhunk Club as it stands today. This is one of the few old bassing club quarters still in existence.

supply came in 1921, when commercial seiners began to pick up stripers in their nets not only off New England, but also off New Jersey and New York. A scattered few anglers north of Chesapeake Bay took fish also in the late 1920s and early 1930s, but these catches for the most part were incidental to seeking other species, such as weakfish and bluefish. However, in 1936 huge schools of small stripers of the two- to three-pound class appeared during the early summer from the Virginia Capes through Maine and into Nova Scotian waters. It was the dawn of another golden age, but not one comparable to the tremendous, still-building boom in striper fishing that got under way immediately following World War II.

In 1946, thanks to relative affluence, more rapid transportation, and a burgeoning desire for adventure on earth's last frontier, a vast host of one-time inland anglers swarmed lemminglike to the sea.

These newcomers lacked the handicaps engendered by the "what's good enough for father is good enough for me" syndrome. Brash and innovative, they promptly experimented with beefed-up versions of lures originated on sweet water and with tactics never before tested under wheeling sea birds. It wasn't long before tradition-oriented old salts found it necessary to step lively in order to compete and then to add their own great leap forward in both tackle and strategy.

After initial stockings of 435 striped bass in 1879 and 1881, California's San Francisco area prospered to such an extent that sport and commercial anglers harvested great numbers of striped warriors throughout the early years of the twentieth century.

The Cuttyhunk Club flagpole sports a carved striped bass at its top.

Many of these early gamesters were taken on bottom baits—just as they were, and still are, in Atlantic waters—for the boom in the use of artificial lures was yet to be triggered on either seaboard. Metal squids were used by Pacific pioneers, many of whom were transplanted Easterners. Like their cousins in New England, New York, and the Chesapeake Bay area, Californians maintained the pace of development and swiftly added local techniques of importance on every striper coast.

Are these to be considered "the early days"? Maybe not, if inscribed on the long roll of history; yet lots of men and women who were considered beach and boat regulars in the late 1940s are now viewed as legendary aces. As this is written, the pioneers of the post-war years are either well into middle age or they have made their last casts prior to fishing around the bend. A new and ardent order of disciples currently forge tomorrow's "Remember when?"

2 · The Fish

CLAIMS HAVE BEEN MADE THAT THE STRIPED BASS AS a species has been researched by marine biologists to the point of absurdity, including minute details of everything from its love life to parasites that chew on it. It is true that there are many hundreds of scientific papers on the species yet, amazingly enough, the vast majority of these are parochial in nature. Most deal with local observations, and all too few give a broad overview of the species throughout its range. Some reports have even been written from a political point of view to support particular legislation or management programs for the fishery in a specific area.

A good fisherman must know his quarry and its habits, so a summary of present knowledge is in order. The physical appearance of this remarkable fish would not indicate that it can make strong men weep and scientists tear their hair in frustration. The description of the bass by biologists as an elongate and little-compressed creature to the layman indicates a fish-shaped fish, neither very long and lean, nor very short and stout. Stripers are inclined to have a pot-bellied look in old age. Excessively thin specimens, which are either on a hunger strike or are wasted by disease, normally are cataloged as racers by fishermen.

The pronounced stripes, usually seven or eight in number, along the sides set this gamester apart from any others sought by salt water anglers. In fresh water, smaller specimens may be confused in southern areas with the white bass, and a cross between these two species has produced a hybrid that combines the characteristics of both species. The color of the stripes and the whole dorsal area varies tremendously in the true striped bass, as was noted by Genio Scott years ago.

"This fish, so beautiful and gamesome, is peculiar to the tidal waters and estuaries of rivers which empty on the coast of the Atlantic from Portland to Norfolk," he wrote. "The striped bass is known further north and south, but it exists in the most perfect state in the rivers along the coast between the points named. . . . Striped bass will live and increase when confined to fresh water, but its shape then becomes changed, and instead of its symmetry and lustre when having access to both fresh and salt waters, it becomes more chubbed, and its color less scintillant."

The striped bass.

Striped bass are somewhat chameleonlike in that they automatically change base color to ensure camouflage. Those taken from deep water usually exhibit dark blue-green backs shading to silvery, iridescent flanks and white bellies. Stripes are then sharply delineated and nearly black. Within 20 minutes or possibly less of moving into a shallow, sandy area, the fish assumes a pale, overall straw color. The back fades to olive and the stripes become brown.

Stripers that are almost orange in color have been reported from the Hudson River in New York to the Maine coast. These specimens do not seem to have the strength of their compatriots of more normal hue and appear to feed mostly on or near the bottom. No satisfactory explanation of the cause for this particular color phase has been forthcoming. They are not confined to one particular geographical area and freely mingle with other fish of more normal coloration.

So different in appearance from their fellows are some bass that many consider river fish a different breed entirely from the surf feeders. This distinction among various types of stripers has been verified by marine biologists who have discovered that there are various races or sub-species with different fin-ray counts and different behavioral patterns. For example, bass that spawn in the Hudson River in New York rarely travel great distances from that river's mouth. Their coloring is brownish in contrast to the silvery-green migrators that move northward from Chesapeake Bay each spring.

It should be noted that almost all of the Canadian bass have broken stripes rather than continuous ones. These fish breed in streams feeding the Saint Lawrence watershed, in the Minas Bay area of Nova Scotia, and in many rivers associated with Atlantic salmon in Nova Scotia, New Brunswick, and Quebec. Striped bass have also been taken from Prince Edward Island waters, but whether this is local stock or not is an unanswered question.

This bass, taken in Maine waters, shows the broken stripes typical of so many stripers caught in Canadian waters. It may well have migrated south and west.

Juvenile stripers are often mistaken for other marine fishlets and vice versa. When very small—less than three inches overall—the youngsters have no stripes at all, while various salt water minnows *do* have them. Hatching grounds for bass are reported each year by eager amateur biologists, but examination of these "striped bass" usually reveals that the hatch was one of striped mummichogs, killifish, or white perch.

Only in the Chesapeake Bay area and parts of the Carolinas can the species be confused with another creature because of popular nomenclature. For generations Bay watermen have called the fish "rock" or "rockfish." It seems unlikely that these highly individualistic fishermen will change their linguistic habits, even though others consider the term "striped bass" as the correct one.

"Missuckeke-kequock" was the name given by American Indians. Like "squidhound" and "greenhead," the term has passed into history. "Linesides" is still encountered when an author is trying not to repeat himself in the same paragraph, and anglers coin a variety of descriptive terms when a bass surges out of control to smash expensive tackle. "Bull bass" is often applied to a large striper, even though heavyweights are all females and should be termed "cows." The definition of "school fish" or "schoolie" varies geographically; it is perhaps most often applied to any catch under ten pounds, that is, a small bass. Where length limits apply, any undersized fish is likely to be dubbed a "short," and in many areas a small one is contemptuously labeled—a description we dislike—a "rat."

For the technically minded, *Roccus lineatus* was for many years the approved Latin. A taxonomist discovered a Mediterranean fish which had been christened by the same title earlier in history, so the American species was tagged *Roccus saxatilis*. Like *Salmo* for the Atlantic salmon, *Roccus* was among the few Latin names to become popular among laymen, yet taxonomists working in Italy were not content. Presumably they had never seen a striper in the wild, but they switched the Latin classification to *Morone saxatilis*, where it remains today—unless another group of taxonomists are huddled over their files intent on producing a new "standard" name next Thursday. For many old-time anglers, *Roccus* still stands!

Attempts have been made to introduce striped bass to continents other than North America but, as of this writing, none has been successful. However, stocking the species in all sorts of odd places in the United States appears to have been a common pastime during the last part of the nineteenth century. The fish were dropped into rivers and ponds, carried from one estuary to another by train and cart, and, in short, given every opportunity to increase and multiply where they had never multiplied before.

The high point of these early efforts came in 1879 when some young stripers were seined from the Navesink River in New Jersey and transported across the continent to San Francisco Bay. This original shipment was augmented by another in 1881. To read the account of this transcontinental trip is an experience in itself. Tank cars as we know them today were not available and the water in huge tubs had to be replenished along the way, agitated by hand by means of a paddle on a geared shaft to keep the young fish alive, and tended with the greatest of care on a 24-hour basis. When crossing the Mississippi, the man tending the tanks at the time tossed a couple of his charges off the railroad trestle into the turgid river "for luck."

How lucky he was can be seen from the fact that the 435 striped bass liberated on the Californian coast increased their numbers to such an extent that the net catch in 1899 alone amounted to 1,234,000 pounds. In 1915, a peak was reached with a marketed total of 1,784,448 pounds.

No one can tell what the number of bass may be on the Pacific Coast today, for commercial netting and sale of the species was stopped by law in California in 1935 and the striper has been classified as a true game fish ever since. The original planting has, however, extended to cover a major portion of the West Coast from San Diego and Orange counties in California north to Oregon. Stragglers have been reported even beyond those limits.

This species is also found on the Atlantic Coast as far south as the Saint Johns River in Florida. However, like most of the stripers ranging south of the Carolinas, the stocks—called southern riverine by scientists—appear to live almost entirely within the river systems and rarely venture beyond the estuaries. In the Gulf of Mexico, there are similar populations, all primarily riverine. The Coosa and Tallapoosa Rivers in Alabama, for example, yield many bass each season, some weighing more than 40 pounds, to anglers fishing hundreds of miles from salt water. Closer to the Gulf itself, such rivers as the Apalachicola in Florida provide sport both in the rivers themselves and in their estuaries. The Gulf race, or races, evidently were isolated following the Ice Age, when waters receded and cut them off from their former haunts. Unrecorded stockings in the late 1800s may also have augmented the supply of bass inland.

Modern stocking programs have been undertaken in estuarine waters of the Gulf. For example, in 1968 a stocking program was started in Chocta-whatchee Bay in Florida and more than 600,000 stripers were introduced. In Mississippi, a continuing program in the Biloxi Bay and Bay Saint Louis areas has resulted in the establishment of a viable fishery for anglers in the river systems feeding those bays. An interesting development in these last named programs is the fact that the bass appear to be moving out into the open Gulf. Tagging returns have been received from Louisiana and elsewhere in the vast tracts of marshland in the delta areas. It seems evident that in years to come, striped bass fishing will become a major factor on the angling scene along most of the Gulf Coast.

On the Atlantic seaboard, striped bass, as noted, range from Florida to the Gulf of the Saint Lawrence. Between these limits, they may be found in

A marine biologist takes a scale sample from a bass prior to releasing it.

the most widely divergent types of water imaginable—from the muddy, warm, fresh, impounded mass of Lakes Moultrie and Marion in South Carolina to the crashing, clear, cold surf of Popham Beach in Maine.

North and east of Maine, Canadian stripers do not wander widely, although in years when bass are unusually abundant to the south, their numbers are augmented by migrators from the northern United States. Like the riverine fish of the Gulf of Mexico, the bass of the Saint Lawrence watershed make short journeys up and down the river system, yet rarely leave the Gulf of the Saint Lawrence itself. Similar local populations were found in many river systems of Nova Scotia, New Brunswick, and Quebec. After spawning, these Canadian stocks in general move almost exactly opposite to their United States cousins—that is, they swim south in the summer and north as waters cool in the autumn.

Stocking of striped bass in fresh water has become commonplace since the 1960s. Where the supply of forage species is high, bass will often thrive and bring an impoundment overpopulated by bait fish back into ecological balance. Improvements in hatchery techniques have resulted in the establishment of the species in fresh water far from any ocean environment in such states as Kansas, Nebraska, and Oklahoma. Man-made Lake Havasu on the Colorado River now yields stripers weighing more than 45 pounds, thanks to stocking that started in 1959.

The inspiration for many of these inland plantings was a remarkable side effect of power dam construction in 1941, when the huge reservoirs of Lake

Moultrie and Lake Marion were sealed off on the Santee–Cooper River system near Moncks Corner in South Carolina. Fisheries biologists realized that some striped bass, native to the two rivers, had been trapped behind the new dams and virtually landlocked. They felt that, after a few years, these survivors would die out. However, almost 300,000 individual fish averaging better than five pounds apiece were taken by anglers in 1957. Obviously the fish were not only holding their own, but were spawning successfully! This fishery has continued to the present day, with fluctuations in supply apparently dependent to a large degree upon the abundance of a food supply consisting of threadfin and gizzard shad. Eyed eggs, fry, and fingerlings obtained from these fresh water stripers have been shipped all over the United States to establish populations where the species has never been seen before, thereby producing a group of inland anglers as fanatical as their coastal brethren.

An earlier source of river-oriented stock was a hatchery established on the Roanoke River at Weldon, North Carolina. Here "rock fights," as the striper spawning activity each spring was termed in early days, were well known. The hatchery has had its ups and downs caused in part by river pollution and in part by budgetary constraints. However, many of the techniques developed at Weldon were the foundations upon which present striped bass culture were laid.

When the colonists at Plymouth, Massachusets, decreed in 1670 that all income from the sale of striped bass, mackerel, and herring taken in the region be set aside to establish a free school for children, spawning runs of stripers evidently were common in a great many rivers flowing into the Atlantic Ocean. Because of dam construction, water pollution, habitat destruction due to coastal development, and perhaps overfishing when local stocks were low, this is no longer the case. There may be some scattered spawning in a few rivers along the Atlantic seaboard of the United States north of the Virginia Capes, but only in the Hudson River in New York and in some tributaries of Delaware Bay does production reach significant proportions. Little is known at this time about the Delaware Bay stocks except that they exist.

Actual spawning takes place with considerable surface commotion. Normally, several males attend a single female and often butt the object of their affection to speed up extrusion of ripe eggs. The eggs, about pinhead size, have a specific gravity slightly greater than fresh water and will remain suspended in a current or even in quiet, brackish water. The warmer the water, the greater the speed of hatching. Thus in 54°F. water, it takes about 80 hours for the larvae to emerge and in 72°F. water, only about 30 hours.

Typical spawning grounds are near the mouths of tidal rivers. The newly hatched stripers spend their first months of life in fresh or brackish water away from the shoreline; when they reach the length of about three inches, they move inshore in schools to feed. In their second summer of life, when their length has doubled, they drop down to saltier waters in the sounds and bays near the rivers of their birth.

Growth rate is rapid in a striper's early years as can be seen from the accompanying graph. This fact originally gave rise to the 16-inch snout-to-fork length limit recommendation. The recommendation was not made because the fish reaches spawning age at that length, but because the species grows more rapidly between the limits of 12 inches and 18 inches than at any other time in its life cycle. Economically, therefore, it makes more sense to harvest 16-inchers; there is more edible flesh and less waste when individual bass are allowed to grow an additional six months. Although male stripers reach sexual maturity in their second year at the length of about 13 inches, females normally must be four years old, or more than 18 inches long. Mature females produce anywhere from 62,000 to 112,000 eggs per pound of body weight.

A popular misconception is that wintering striped bass, found in many river systems, are spawning. That is not the case. Bass that winter over in any given area *may* spawn the next spring, yet many do not. Stripers do not develop eggs and milt every year as a fixed rule, nor do they necessarily migrate every year. An individual specimen may spend the cold season in a certain locality simply because the area appeals to its fishy personality.

Relationship between age and size can be determined quite accurately by scale readings of bass until they grow to 25 pounds. Each year an annulus, similar to the ring of growth in a tree, is formed. As the fish grow larger, distinguishing the annuli becomes more difficult. Thus the 73-pounder that stood as the record rod-and-reel catch for many years after it was caught in 1913 by Charles B. Church on an eel bait off the Elizabeth Islands in Massachusetts, might have been anywhere from 31 to 40 years old. The two huge bass weighing 125 pounds apiece in the round and caught in 1891 by a seiner near Edenton, North Carolina, may well have celebrated their golden anniversaries. It is also possible, as is true of so-called "giants" among humans, that they suffered from some glandular trouble.

It is interesting to note that the top weight limits of rod-and-reel catches have changed by only a few pounds over the decades. The International Game Fish Association set aside Church's catch because of uncertainty about the strength of the line used. Its place was taken by a 72-pounder caught by Edward J. Kirker off Cuttyhunk, Massachusetts, on October 10, 1969. Another 73-pounder was boated by Charles E. Cinto on June 16, 1967, in the same area, but was disqualified under IGFA rules because wire line was used. On November 3, 1981, Tony Stetzko of Orleans, Massachusetts, broke all surf fishing records by beaching yet another 73-pounder on 20-pound-test line while fishing the outer beaches of Cape Cod.

Latest among the rod-and-reel monsters to break the all-tackle record was one of 76 pounds hooked just after an eclipse of the moon in the early hours of July 17, 1981, by Robert Rocchetta, a policeman in Suffolk County,

New York. The bait was a live eel drifted near Eastern Rock about a mile east of Montauk Point at the tip of Long Island. The Church, Kirker, and Rocchetta bass all fell for eels and Stetzko's fish gobbled a Black Beauty fly fished as a dropper in front of an eel. Eels obviously are a favorite food among big stripers at all seasons.

Probably the largest striper ever reported caught by any means was a fish netted in 1915 off Worton Point in the upper Chesapeake Bay by Captain Charles O. Cummings, a commercial fisherman. The fish's weight, *minus head, tail, roe, and entrails*, was 106 pounds. Marine biologists estimate that the missing parts would have weighed at least 38 pounds, which would have brought this gigantic striper's weight to an amazing 144 pounds! There is little question that bass of 100 pounds or better still are swimming in the oceans and bays, but chances of taking them on rod and reel are slim. After

A close-up of a pug-nosed bass, a 12-pounder caught on Cape Cod.

all, they have reached their huge size by knowing how to avoid danger and, even if hooked, may be difficult to horse away from a barnacle-covered rock or other obstruction dedicated to parting all connections between angler and fish.

Tall tales about huge fish in the "good old days" will not stand the hard scrutiny of facts. Genio P. Scott, previously mentioned, set the average striper taken by the anglers of 1870 in New York and New England waters at about 17 pounds. The late Dr. John H. Cunningham of Massachusetts, who obtained records of three bassing clubs located at Cuttyhunk, Pasque, and Squibnocket and covering the period from 1865 to 1915, noted that the average size was almost five pounds less. The largest specimen reported in those records weighed 62 pounds—a record that has been broken many times between 1958 and the present.

As is true among many species of fish, as a particular year's class goes through its cycle of years, survivors tend to become fewer and fewer, yet larger and larger. Natural mortality, plus harvesting by fishermen, reduces the population to comparatively few survivors of great weight. These are the record breakers.

Like any other creature in the world, a striper's rate of growth depends a good deal on what it eats—and it will eat just about anything, including its own kind. Crabs, eels, small fish of all kinds, various shellfish, sea worms large and small, squid, shrimp, even small jellyfish and sea cabbage, all have been found in the stomachs of bass. There is one case on record of a Thames River angler in Connecticut who saw a young fish swallow a carelessly flipped cigarette butt!

Anglers are not content to use the many hundreds of natural baits at their disposal, however. They have dreamed up magnificent creations of metal and nylon, wood, feathers, rope, plastic, and glass that would bring a blush to the brow of a modernistic interior decorator. And, when the spirit moves them, bass engulf any or all of these offerings. Unfortunately for the fisherman, the spirit does not always move. Stripers feed heavily for short periods, then rest and digest for much longer periods. This habit makes them the maddening and fascinating quarry that they are.

One fact which many fishermen forget is that the feeding habits of large bass are different than those of small ones. There are occasions when big fish will school in the surf or in a tide rip—usually just prior to the autumn migrations—slashing and cutting at every smidgeon of bait in the area; but for the most part, they leave such brisk activity to the youngsters under 20 pounds.

Very big bass are apt to cruise singly, in pairs, or in small pods, feeding where the living is easy. With their blunt snouts, they will root in soft mud or sand, expelling bursts of water to dislodge shellfish and crustaceans before cracking the unfortunate bait in their powerful jaws. Rather than seek out minnows and other small fish, these lazy monsters often lie behind a rock in a current and let the meal swim to them. They prefer a big mouthful to a snack, so the basic rule that large baits or lures catch large fish is a good one.

Watching stripers feed in shallow water is an education in itself. We once saw both large and small bass dining on eels as the black squirmers were swept out through the mouth of a tidal pond. The young fish would swim up behind their intended victim and try to engulf it tail-first. This worked well enough with small eels, but the large ones invariably wriggled free. Big bass picked only the big eels, swam by them, and in passing, dealt the bait a terrific blow with their tails. Before a stunned eel could regain control, the striper would turn and bolt it down head-first. Such tactics are not limited to feeding on eels: big fish stun all types of swimming ocean creatures that otherwise might move out of range, then eat them in a comparatively leisurely manner.

A North Carolina striper fell victim to a goosefish (ocean angler). Photo by Aycock Brown.

Moral: If you feel a tap on a lure or bait, drop it back as though it had been stunned. The bass may well return to gobble it down.

Striped bass are selective feeders. This means simply that they will choose one type of food rather than another if the choice is offered, just as a wine connoisseur prefers vintage champagne to sparkling cider. This selectivity can be exasperating, to say the least. Take the case of an angler who sees big stripers knocking small menhaden out of the water, attaches a lure that looks like the menhaden, but coaxes nary a strike. Although he cannot be sure, the angler immediately suspects that the bass are not feeding on the acrobatic mossbunkers, but on some other bait swimming with them. The problem calls for rapid identification of the preferred delicacy so that it can be matched with an artificial lure.

In addition to selectiveness, bass follow no set pattern of regular feeding. In obeying their own strange instincts, the fish may drive into action at any time, day or night. Dawn and dusk are favored hours, however, and the deep night often brings stripers close to shore. That is when the fanatic surf caster, slipping and crawling over weed-draped rocks, his pockets bulging and sodden with rigged eels, considers himself close to paradise!

Morning, noon, or night—high tide, half tide, or dead low—stripers flurry when conditions please them. Just when the angling fraternity believes it has discovered the exact time (double-checked by moon phase, wind direction, barometer, and tide) to fish, these striped furies change their feeding schedule. We remember one of those unexpected rampages: It erupted at high noon of a hot August day—and the tide was at flat ebb!

There are a few generalities that hold more or less true. Normally in open water and along the surf line, the top two hours of flood tide produce the best results. Spring tides, when both sun and moon exert gravitational pull on the oceans in the same direction, are apt to provide better fishing than neap tide periods. Note that, when the moon is full, bass may feed all night by its light, with the result that daytime fishing drops off. The dying away of a northerly blow is favored by striper anglers of the Northeast, but in more southern waters a dying southeaster is preferred. However, we never say always: These are generalities that have merit; they are not infallible.

Studying the feeding habits of the striper will bring more fish to beach or boat. Opening up the first fish of the day and examining the stomach contents pays dividends. Just as a trout fisherman matches the hatch of insects when selecting flies, so can a bass angler identify the meal of the moment and pick a lure that duplicates it as closely as possible.

Tides, winds, and temperatures all have their effects and a good fisherman learns the consequences of these effects in his own area. He also learns to recognize likely-looking spots for bass—a mussel bed here, a deep hole there, perhaps a break in an offshore bar or a mud flat where cruising stripers root for sea worms. Neophytes may assume that one bit of ocean, bay, or river

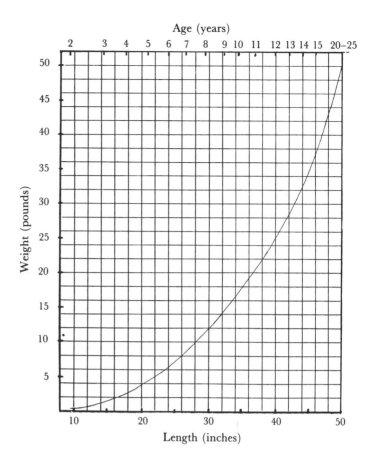

Age (years)

Weight (pounds)

Length (inches)

This graph shows the relation of age to length and weight for the average striped bass. It is most accurate for smaller fish.

looks, and therefore is, just like another, but the experienced basser entertains no such illusions. The beach may be unfamiliar, yet he heads for the best location, the spot that qualifies as "good water."

And what makes good water? It is impossible to list all of the details taken into consideration by a striper-conscious salt water angler as he scans the fishing grounds. So many factors, so many imponderables are concerned, that experience must be the leavening agent. There are, however, a few general rules which may serve as basic guides. First, striped bass prefer to lie in a current and, like many other robust game fish, they are apt to feed where the current is strong and active, and rest where the flow is relatively gentle. From the time that they are fertile eggs until they die, moving water is the choice of the bass.

Boiling tide rips, spots where waves break or nearly break over sand bars and rocks, deep holes into which feed is washed, mouths of tidal rivers where fresh and salt waters clash—all of these are likely spots. Where whitecaps and spray dash high into the air, where surf and wind combine to produce lively water, there school fish may be found. Big bass will occasionally move into such water, but in general the deeper, darker currents are their favorites.

Clarity of water is another important factor, yet one that is relative and often misunderstood. Bits of weed and goglum may bother an angler, but this sort of suspended matter troubles fish little. However, silt and cloudiness, mud and roiled sand, will often drive bass offshore or stop them from feeding. Clarity is, of course, comparative. The clearest water ever seen in the Pungo

River in North Carolina contains more matter in suspension than the cloud-iest water on record for the Parker River in Massachusetts, but a compara-tively clear condition on either stream produces the best sport fishing.

Every striper addict has his favorite spot. To name and describe every one of these would fill a volume twice this size, and the work would be out of date before it was printed. Regions where fishing has been good in the past and will probably be good in the future are indicated in the appendix of this book and discussed in the chapters which pertain to migrations and tech-niques of fishing. Local concentrations are ably plotted by the rod and gun writers of daily newspapers and by television and radio reporters. Watch the weather and the tides; make friends with a local angler who is out every day and most of the night. Then do as we do—go fishing whenever you get the chance.

No secret lure, trick, or bit of information withheld from the average angler makes a successful striped bass fisherman. The true expert studies his fish and the waters where that fish lives. Only study, coupled with the facility to note and accept change, makes one angler a better fisherman than his neighbors. Somewhere, back in the complex file of memory, the successful basser stores a potpourri of small observations. Sea lice on a caught striper are not just water bugs; they are sure indication that the beached fish comes from a fairly large school. Birds wheeling and dipping close astern of an approach-ing boat are not a sign of fish; the boatman is simply disposing of trash or cleaning his catch. So the details add up: the look of good water, the tendency of fish to feed when the wind is in a certain quarter, the build-up of a tide rip. No answer is ever absolute, no angler is ever completely successful. That is why striped bass fishermen are a race apart—they match wits and gear against one of the most unpredictable warriors of the sea.

3 · Migrations, Multitudes, and Management

"THE STRIPED BASS IS NOT MIGRATORY, BEING found along our coasts in winter as well as in summer, and in our markets every month of the year."

So wrote Professor George Brown Goode and his co-authors in *The Fisheries and Fishery Industries of the United States*, an extraordinarily comprehensive tome published in 1884 by the United States Government. Because bass were so plentiful in many different river systems, the belief that the species was basically a local fish, and that the total coastwide supply was made up of many separate populations, was a common one. There is some truth in this premise, but the non-migratory statement is incorrect.

In 1936, Daniel Merriman, later to become a professor in his own right at Yale University, started tagging stripers in the vicinity of the Niantic River in Connecticut. During the next two years, this program expanded. His findings and recommendations were published in final form by the U. S. Fish and Wildlife Service in 1941: *Studies on the Striped Bass (Roccus Saxatilis) of the Atlantic Coast*. Merriman explored the factors involved in cycles of abundance and scarcity of the fish, came forward with the 16-inch length limit we mentioned earlier, and, most important, proved that stripers do migrate seasonally in many cases.

Since his original work, continuing research involving both tagging and meristic studies—differences in fin-ray counts and the like—has shown clearly that some striped bass migrate over great distances and that the patterns of these migrations may vary considerably from year to year. In general, however, traveling bass, like bathing beauties, follow the sun. During winter months when water temperatures are low, stripers remain rather inactive.

An example of this almost dormant condition was made clear during the 1930s in the Parker River in Massachusetts. Commercial fishermen would cut a channel across the river ice just below a known bass wintering hole. A large bow net was then lowered through this slot and a can full of acid was dropped into the water upstream through another cut in the ice. As the current carried the acid to the fish, they would float blinded and gasping into the waiting net. Such methods virtually annihilated the native population in the Parker.

In general, striped bass become active when water warms to about 45°F. and in the spring start to think about food and the opposite sex. Note also that fish that migrate south in the autumn start their journey when waters are at the same temperature. Spawning takes place in water that is between 53° and 60°F. Large bass appear to prefer temperatures around 68°F., while their smaller relatives choose an aquatic climate a degree or two higher for normal living and feeding. When the water hits 80°F. they move out. With this information tucked away in an angler's memory, a thermometer can be a very useful adjunct to fishing tackle.

For spawners, migrations start after they have dropped eggs or milt in the spring. Younger bass get the wanderlust earlier and thus the first fish to hit the coast along the Atlantic migratory routes are what are commonly termed "schoolies." These youngsters also are the last to leave northern waters in the autumn on their return trip south. For reasons unknown, their journey to New England and the Canadian Provinces are more extensive than those of the large adults during the late spring and summer months.

The primary source of migrating bass along the northeastern Atlantic Coast is Chesapeake Bay. This does not mean that all fish in those waters move out into the open ocean between the Virginia Capes and head north in the spring when they reach traveling age of between 12 and 14 inches. In the James River, for example, there appears to be a breed of bass that rarely travels outside the confines of the Bay during its entire life cycle. As more studies have been conducted, it has become evident that migrations, both those that are fairly local in nature and those that cover hundreds of miles, are far more complicated than was first supposed.

Very large bass are taken every winter along the Outer Banks of North Carolina and further south on the Carteret coast. They congregate from late November well into January, and there are few fish weighing less than 15 pounds in these schools. For many years, these fish were taken only by seiners, but, since the late 1970s, more and more have been beached by anglers. These bass may well be the breeding stock that supply rivers flowing into Albemarle and Pamlico Sounds. However, during the month of February, long before spawning season, similar schools of huge fish gather at the mouth of the Potomac River in Chesapeake Bay. Whether or not these fish are from the wintering schools of North Carolina, no one is sure.

Emphasis should be placed on the fact that migrants from Virginia and Maryland waters do not necessarily make the long swim every year. Although hard proof is lacking at this time, it seems evident that some stripers, particularly those of the four- and five-pound class, may remain out of Chesapeake Bay for two or three years before returning to their birthplace. To complicate matters even more, highly migratory specimens intermingle with riverine stocks, such as those found in New York's Hudson River. Some apparently winter over with their new found friends.

Although general migratory routes of the travelers from the Chesapeake and other basic supply sources have been delineated as the accompanying map shows, these routes are not by any means fixed. In 1980, for example, a great many stripers weighing up to 20 pounds and more moved inland on their way south during the autumn run. A few—a very few—anglers made a killing on these fish in the East River in New York and around Governor's Island for nearly two weeks. At the same time, another small group of fishermen found bass of all sizes just a few miles west of the edge of Georges Bank in Massachusetts and, a little later, off Maryland near the western edge of the Gulf Stream. It is possible that this change from the normal coastal pattern of travel was caused by the fact that hordes of bluefish provided too much competition for the food supply and that the slower-moving stripers simply moved to where living was easier. Bass and bluefish are found together, but the more aggressive blues often cause stripers to move elsewhere to feed.

Migrations from the Chesapeake Bay area normally start in April and by the end of that month the first bright fish—so-called to distinguish them from bass that have wintered over—have reached waters south of Cape Cod in Massachusetts. From that time forward, the number of migrants continues to increase, larger specimens following the schoolies. These big fish are all females, for the male bass rarely grows to a weight of more than 15 pounds. The ratio of males to females among the migrants apparently decreases as the fish move further north. In Maine, for example, random sampling produces only one male to every 20 females, although much more research on this point is needed to establish a sound baseline.

By mid-May, stripers are feeding throughout their entire range and good fishing for both migrants and local populations continues through June. Weather conditions and the availability of forage species then become more and more important as far as anglers are concerned. A long stretch of hot, dry weather often results in bass seeking deep water and hitting primarily after dark. In the late 1950s and early 1960s, August doldrums were accepted as a matter of angling fact. However, development of new techniques, such as wire-line trolling, has shown that stripers are still available and may be caught even during this slack period.

By mid-August, things start to pick up in the northern part of the striper's range as the fish begin to feed heavily, instinctively stockpiling the energy needed to take them south or to move on to wintering grounds. From Nova Scotia and the Saint Lawrence River down through southern Rhode

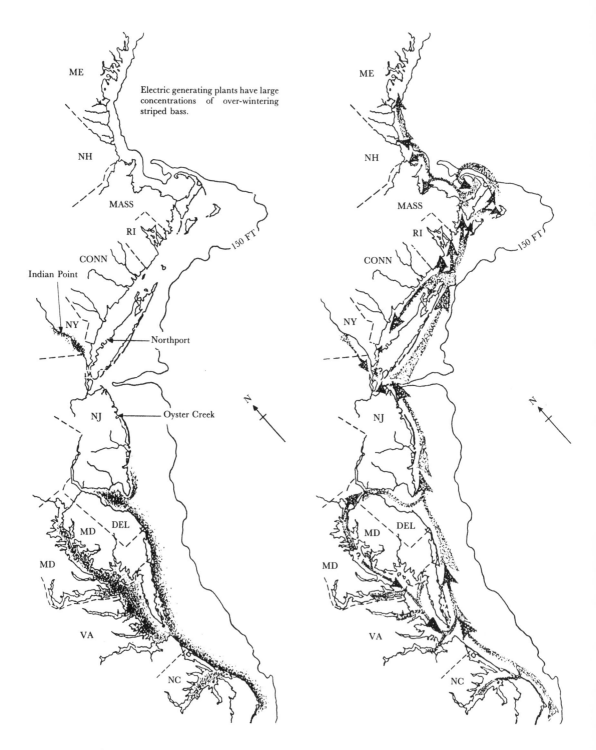

Figure 1. *Overwintering (December to February) locations and relative abundance of striped bass along the Middle Atlantic and New England coasts.* Figure 2. *Spring (March to May) migratory routes of striped bass along the Middle Atlantic and New England coasts.*

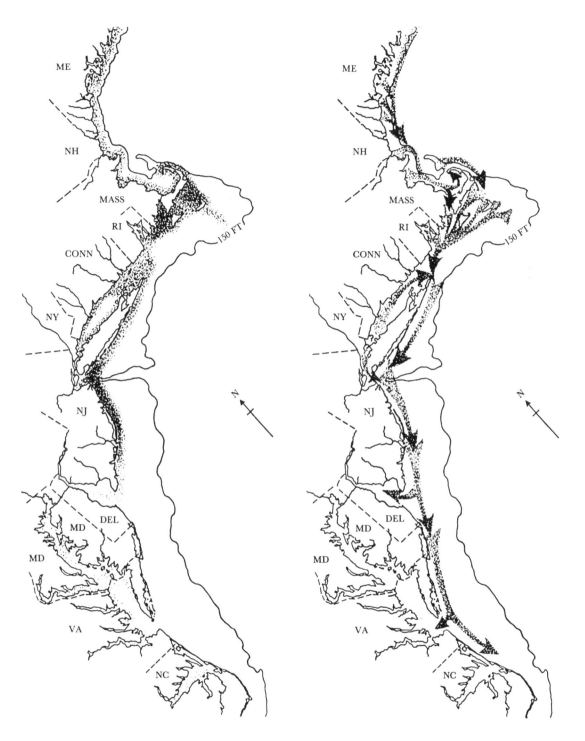

Figure 3. *Summering (June to August) locations and relative abundance of striped bass along the Middle Atlantic and New England coasts*. Figure 4. *Fall (September to November) migratory routes of striped bass along the Middle Atlantic and New England coasts*.

Island, September and early October are conceded to be the best fishing season. This early fall period is also productive from Montauk Point on New York's Long Island down through Georgia.

As might be expected, peak periods occur later in the season as migrants move down the coast. Thus, catches along the Long Island and New Jersey shores are best during October and often well into November. In Chesapeake Bay itself, late autumn is a prime time for bassing. The Bay Bridge and Tunnel structure, running from Cape Henry to Cape Charles in Virginia, provides some excellent fishing for large bass through most of December. When the line storms of late fall hit, however, striped bass fishing may be considered over for all practical purposes from Delaware Bay northwards.

In some specific spots, such as Old Man Rip off the coast of Nantucket in Massachusetts, bass of all sizes often gang up in huge schools just before they start south. Whipped by autumn winds, such rips can provide some of the fastest fishing imaginable, and some of the most rugged. The bonanza may last for only a day or two, or for as long as two weeks. While it does last, gorging stripers will hit almost any lure presented. The trick is to locate such hot spots; unfortunately, the locality may change from one year to the next.

Over and above the abundance and scarcity caused by migrating striped bass along the eastern seaboard are cycles caused by successful or unsuccessful spawning in any given year. Such cycles have been going on since the striper was first sought by early colonists—and even before white men arrived on the North American continent, according to several specialists in Indian culture. A look at history almost a hundred years ago illustrates the point.

"Canadian authorities inform us that, though the bass still occur along the New Brunswick and Nova Scotia shores of the Gulf [of the Saint Lawrence]," George Brown Goode reported in 1884, "they are much less abundant and of smaller size than formerly. . . . The bass fishery in Cape Cod Bay was formerly of great importance, but capture of this fish is now of rare occurrence."

Goode predicted a major decline in the population of striped bass along the northeastern Atlantic seaboard, and he was right. Within a decade, as we noted in the opening chapter, the old bassing clubs closed their doors, stripers apparently vanished except in the Chesapeake Bay area, and rod-and-reel anglers shifted their targets to weakfish and bluefish. With the brood stocks at an apparent all-time low, for reasons yet to be explained a tremendous hatch occurred in 1934—a hatch that established what biologists term a dominant-year class. When these small stripers started to migrate in 1936 and 1937, bass fishing was born again along the entire Atlantic seaboard. A new generation of fanatical anglers was born also.

The ups and downs of the bass supply for a 30-year period are given in the accompanying graph. The decline from 1973 to 1980 was steady, and the big leap in 1973 was due to an extraordinary hatch in 1970, when small stripers began their seasonal migrations.

Despite the fact that sampling of larvae and small bass can be conducted with a fair degree of accuracy on known spawning grounds, final proof of the hatching success is not definitely established until the young fish grow for two or three years to a size large enough to be taken in the sport and commercial fisheries. It is a sort of hindsight operation from the scientific point of view, so that it is difficult even to suggest corrective action until the damage has been done. One factor that contributes to the problem is that sampling of all spawning rivers is impossible due to the time and costs involved.

Cycles of abundance and scarcity in the waters of Chesapeake Bay, Atlantic Coast rivers south of that area, and in Canada have coincided remarkably closely, even though the spawning bass are from different stocks. These cycles also are duplicated to a large degree among the stripers of the Pacific Coast, although the supply of fresh water apparently has been the predominant factor there. The exception to the rule has been the Hudson River in New York; when catches were plunging downwards elsewhere in the late 1970s, they were climbing slightly in the Hudson area. As previously noted, however, these fish do not move out of Long Island Sound or far south of Sandy Hook to any large degree.

Fishermen as a group tend to blame a single cause for the decline in abundance of the quarry they seek. This has been all too true in the case of the

A graph of landings of striped bass over a 30-year period along the northeastern Atlantic coast. Included are the best figures available for commercial catches and estimates of recreational catches.

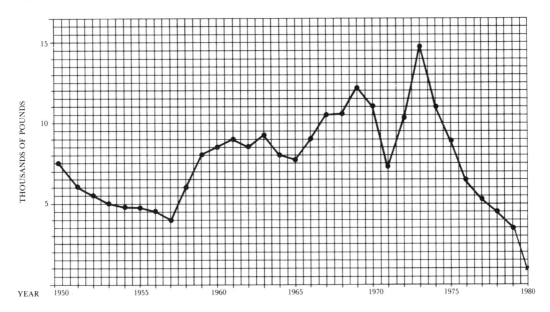

striped bass. One of the earliest targets in the late 1960s for the single-cause group was polychlorinated biphenyls (PCBs), which are known to have a lethal effect upon many living organisms. The presence of PCBs may have been a contributing factor to bass decline, yet stocks in the Hudson River, which is so highly polluted with PCBs that the eating of fish from its waters has been discouraged by the Food and Drug Administration, have survived and multiplied.

Similarly, a single cause of stock decline in the James River, which flows into Chesapeake Bay, did come to light when a tremendous amount of Kepone was introduced into that river with disastrous results to most aquatic life. The striped bass spawning grounds were thought to have been lost forever and the polluted waters were closed to fishing. Oddly enough, this disaster led to a benefit. The James became a virtual sanctuary for bass and the population built back to normal limits rather quickly—and then exceeded them!

There is no question that pollution from waste matter, chemicals, farm fertilizers, and a host of other contaminants can cause damage to both young and old stripers. Similarly, destruction of habitat, including tidal nursery areas and river spawning grounds, can take its toll, yet none of these is the *single* cause of the tremendous cyclic fluctuations in the bass population.

Nature also puts in an oar. In 1978, there were several unexplained kills of bass, particularly in the New York area. After intensive research on dead specimens, it was found that a specific bacterium was present in all of them. When cultured and injected into healthy stripers the bacteria caused almost instant death. What caused the flowering, for want of a better word, of these bacteria? No one knows. It might well be that a major epizootic was triggered by this same type of bacterium at the turn of the century, wiping out bass all along the coast.

Although there are various diseases that afflict stripers from time to time, none appears to have more than a local effect upon the supply. Fin rot is not uncommon in highly polluted waters such as the Hudson River. Cataracts form over the eyes of many wintering fish, particularly in the New England area. This apparently is caused by some dietary deficiency for, when spring comes and the bass start to forage more widely, the cataracts disappear. Deformities, particularly in newly hatched fry, are not uncommon and, although some individual specimens reach maturity with twisted spines or pug-head characteristics, most of these fish die young. Several dozen parasites have been identified in stripers and, as is true of any marine species, the more plentiful the supply of hosts, the more plentiful the numbers of parasites. However, none of these unwelcome guests appear to have enough effect on the overall bass population to cause cycles of scarcity.

Another factor which should be considered when discussing these cycles is the effect of weather at the time the fish are spawning. The flow of fresh

The IGFA all-tackle world's record striped bass. This 76-pounder was taken by Robert Rocchetta on July 17, 1981 east of Montauk Point, New York on a live eel. Photo by Al Ristori.

water on the grounds, the amount of cloud cover, air and water temperatures, all undoubtedly have some influence upon the success of the hatch. Amazingly little research has been done on such environmental conditions, so there is little understanding about what makes ideal circumstances for a peak hatch. If these ideal conditions could be discovered, it might well be possible to simulate them either in hatcheries or at selected sites in the wild.

One indication of the possible importance of such factors came from research done at the University of Maryland's Chesapeake Biological Laboratory. Findings announced in 1981 indicated that a key to dominant-year classes is the abundance of food for larval bass immediately after they have absorbed their yolk sacs and started to feed under their own power. Zooplankton, the microscopic organisms upon which these tiny fish feed, munch in turn upon detritus composed of dead vegetable matter washed into the spawning and nursery rivers and bays from nearby wetlands.

Women's world records caught off North Truro, Massachusetts on August 14, 1960. Kay Townsend, left, displays a 63½-pounder, while her close friend Rosa Webb stands behind her 64½-pound bass. Both fish were hooked on live mackerel baits.

The researchers correlated weather and beach seine records kept over a 25-year period. Ideal conditions, and subsequent dominant-year classes, apparently depend upon below-average winter temperatures starting in December and above-average water levels for a five-day period the following April, when the larvae are starting to feed actively. Cold weather keeps the detritus from rotting away and also freezes it in place. With heavy rains in April, the material is washed into the nursery areas, zooplankton thrives, and young bass thrive also. Although this research was confined to the Potomac River, it may also apply on striper spawning grounds from Chesapeake Bay northwards. Because of a lack of freezing weather of any great duration elsewhere, it would not seem to apply outside these boundaries.

In late 1972, we heard at a seminar concerning striped bass that incubating striper eggs in a hatchery died when an electronic flash unit was used to photograph them. The Lyman-Woolner theory, which holds that predictable amounts of ultraviolet light may destroy eggs and fry on the spawning grounds, was born. After consultation with scientists and astronomers, it was discovered that there was a definite correlation between the times of high

Tony Stetzko of Orleans, Massachusetts with the 73-pound striper he landed on November 3, 1981. It is the largest bass taken by a surf caster to date. Photo by Tony Chiarappo.

sunspot activity, when the earth is bombarded with increased amounts of ultraviolet light, and poor bass hatches. As this is written, a major decrease in sunspot activity is predicted. It will be interesting to note whether or not the hatching success improves in coming years. If it does, we will accept our Nobel prize with all due modesty.

Whatever the cause of these cycles of abundance and scarcity may be, it is highly probable that mankind can do little or nothing about them even after they have been discovered. However, measures certainly can be taken to conserve what bass there are even in a poor-year class and to spread the benefits of a good-year class over a wide period and geographical area.

One of the major handicaps in striped bass management over the years has been the fact that the fish swim across the political boundaries between

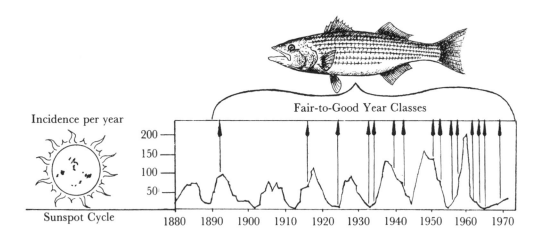

Incidence per year

Fair-to-Good Year Classes

200
150
100
50

Sunspot Cycle

1880 1890 1900 1910 1920 1930 1940 1950 1960 1970

This sunspot graph was compiled by the authors to document their hypothesis about the effect of sunspots on good- or fair-year classes of striped bass.

states. Fifteen Atlantic coast states have striper populations, with the District of Columbia tossed in for good measure. Eleven of these are involved in one way or another in the migrations of bass from Chesapeake Bay. Each state government jealously guards its rights over water within three miles of the coast, and the striper is basically a coastal traveler. Uniformity of laws concerning the legal length of fish taken, bag limits, seasons, closed spawning areas, and all similar measures normally considered in management programs are sadly lacking.

The classic example is the case of a striper migrating out of the Chesapeake to swim north in the spring. Laws are rapidly changing, but in 1980 a 12-inch fish was legal game in Maryland, yet restrictions were placed on any presumed breeders weighing more than 15 pounds. Once they had traveled about 100 miles north, 12-inchers were safe under the law because the 16-inch, or equivalent, limit prevailed in northern states. However, 15-pounders and bass of greater size were fair game. In some states netting was permitted, while in others catches were restricted to hook and line and in some sale was forbidden. In brief, regulations covering the taking of bass were a hodgepodge of contradictions which, overall, could not be justified in any way as sound conservation measures, even though they might have had some merit locally.

Haul seine catches of striped bass such as this one not only destroy many brood stock fish, but also depress the commercial market.

Coordinated action among Atlantic seaboard states to develop a sound management plan for striped bass, to standardize laws and regulations, to fill the gaps in scientific knowledge concerning the species, and, one hopes, to come up with a program that would insure the best use of whatever population of stripers there might be on hand at a given time, started in 1977. Since that date, the program has moved forward despite restraints due to lack of financing. For the first time, federal, state, and private agencies were working together towards common goals.

In late 1981, a special Striped Bass Fishery Management Board, made up of individuals from Maine to North Carolina, came up with recommendations to be incorporated into the interstate striped bass fishery management plan. The plan itself is to be coordinated by the Atlantic States Marine Fisheries Commission, which was established in 1942 by an Act of Congress to insure cooperation among a variety of state agencies dealing with marine fisheries of all sorts. Although it may take several years before the recommendations are implemented and the effects noted on the striper population, at least there now is, at long last, a firm structure upon which to build.

Among the recommendations approved were the following: Minimum keeping size for bass in the Hudson River, Chesapeake Bay, and North Carolina's Albermarle Sound will be 14 inches, snout to fork of tail. Elsewhere, the minimum size will be 24 inches. (There is a long-established market for the smaller fish in the areas where the 14-inch limit was set.)

Typical school-sized striped bass taken on light spinning tackle.

In addition, all major spawning areas, as designated by the states involved, will be closed during the spawning season. All persons who buy or sell striped bass would be required to obtain a permit. A monitoring and data collection program will be implemented to define the fishery further and to study the effect of the management plan.

These are the bare bones of the program as this is written. It may bring the extraordinary fluctuations in the Atlantic coast bass supply under some semblance of control. Until that day, the striper fisherman watches the tides, phases of the moon, and even the sun—spots and all. He lives on hope, with perhaps a fish or two thrown in for good measure.

In California, the problem is far more basic—water. Lack of fresh water, the pumping of it from northern to southern California, the destruction wrought by the pumps themselves and by screening systems at the pump intakes, all had brought the striped bass population down to an estimated one million fish in 1981—a drop of approximately 70 percent within two decades. Some biologists have stated that the fishery is doomed in the San Francisco Bay and Delta areas unless some immediate action is taken to correct the dearth of water in which bass may live and breed.

Eggs and small stripers in huge quantities are sucked into the California Aqueduct and Delta Mendota Canal to furnish much-needed irrigation to the San Joaquin Valley and to supply the sprawling, growing city of Los Angeles. In addition, California's Department of Water Resources is planning the so-called Peripheral Canal—a project which, if completed, would take water from the Sacramento River at Hood, where bass are not plentiful. The idea is that the pumps now installed near bass concentrations and spawning grounds will be abandoned, but the project, which would take a dozen years to complete at the cost of at least a billion dollars, would still divert water in perhaps even greater volume than at the present rate. Pollution from sewage and pesticides is another contributing factor to the decline in striper populations in the area.

Solutions to these problems are primarily political in nature, with fishermen in the north pitting the value of the fisheries against the agricultural and human demands of those living in the south. Heavy rainfall, so that the severe drought of 1977 is not repeated, plus reasonable compromise between the two factions may bring back bass to their former abundance. There has also been considerable success in the establishment of hatcheries to augment the supply.

In Oregon waters to the north, fishing is concentrated primarily in the Coos Bay and Umpqua River areas. These stripers originally came from the stocking of fish in California waters, yet oddly enough, today there is little exchange between California and Oregon stocks. No commercial fishing for the species is allowed in Oregon and anglers are limited in their efforts through both bag and length restrictions. The fishery depends largely upon successful hatches and resulting dominant-year classes, although there are some pollution problems which may affect both young and adult bass.

Californians who seek stripers pray for rain, hope for better screening of present pump intakes, talk of hatcheries, and curse pollution. It would be a sorry commentary on alleged human progress if they have to turn towards Oregon as a source of striped bass stocks to replenish those which are being destroyed in their own home waters.

4 · Weapons Systems

STRIPED BASS FISHERMEN ARE AT ONCE THE NICEST people in the world and the most intolerant. Your high surf squidder has a tendency to look down his sunburned nose at folk who use boats, and there is a rapidly building legion of ultra-light enthusiasts who rarely wrap their brine-caked paws around anything other than a fly rod, a featherweight spinning outfit, or a baitcasting rig that in the late 1930s might have been dismissed as a tool of the inland angler seeking tiddlers in fresh water.

Add to this list a number of trolling combinations, many of them deemed "practical," meaning relatively heavy, and others balanced to succeed with the lightest of line tests allowed by the International Game Fish Association in salt water record competition. All of the rod-reel-line packages are specialized to a certain extent, and each is worthy of respect.

Striped bass fishing boasts its full share of purists, ladies and gentlemen who feel that their chosen method is the only acceptable way to go. Ideally, a master angler will have studied and participated in each of the disciplines prior to settling on the one that provides greatest personal pleasure. We go down to the sea for high sport, for inner joy and a sense of freedom too often fouled by the weedy waters of business-as-usual in the clattering cities or gossipy suburbs.

Specialization in choice of tackle, together with imaginative sorties into possible new techniques, may be pretty far out, yet lessons learned through trial and error benefit all hands. No Indianapolis speed wagon much resembles a mass-produced automobile spawned in Detroit or Japan, but technical advances proved worthy in hard competition swiftly find their way into the sanitized guts of the highway machines we take for granted.

For something better than half a century, split bamboo was considered the finest of rod building materials. One still sees a few of the old classics on every striper coast, but the hurry-hurry research and technology of World War II entered a new champion in the lists—synthetics. A phase-out of split cane did not occur overnight, but it was progressive. Practically all of today's salt water rods are constructed of fiberglass, graphite, boron, or subtle mixtures of the three.

Heavy surf spinning tackle is favored by many shore casters.

These modern sticks are far lighter than their organic predecessors; they are tougher, require a minimum of maintenance, and lend themselves to manufacturing controls so that precise action is guaranteed by each blank designed for a specific task. These are less expensive than the best of custom-made split bamboo shafts and, to say it simply, far superior in every way, other than in the understandable human reluctance to accept technical advances that fracture youthful dreams.

This was, of course, the beginning of a tackle advance that, in a scant couple of decades, eclipsed all that had been accomplished in a previous century. Three breakthroughs, together with the general upgrading of marine gear, heralded a new era. These were the development of synthetic rod building materials, the advent of spinning as a strong competitor of revolving spool, and swift acceptance of both nylon and dacron lines.

The post-war angling revolution was aided and abetted by a host of feisty inland fishermen who swarmed to the sea immediately after the guns were silenced in the late summer of 1945. These people were young, strong, and innovative. They were not at all bothered by ancient tradition, and they demanded the best of equipment.

Whether or not this infusion of new blood was directly responsible for launching a light tackle trend, history indicates that the "spiderweb crusade" was well underway by the late 1940s. Prior to that time a majority of striped bass fishermen were wedded to stout rod-reel-line combinations, and anyone who appeared on the scene with "buggy whip" gear was mildly viewed as a harmless nut. "Don't knock it," the old stagers grinned. "These guys are conservationists and they leave all the bass for us!"

It was not long before polite scorn was replaced by frowning incredulity and, gradually, to acceptance based on the "If you can't lick 'em, join 'em" school of thought. Big, tough outfits continue to see much service, yet each is far more specialized than the norm of yesteryear. Each is designed to do a certain thing well.

Pictured top to bottom are fly casting, spinning, bait casting, and revolving spool surf casting combinations; all are effective on striped bass.

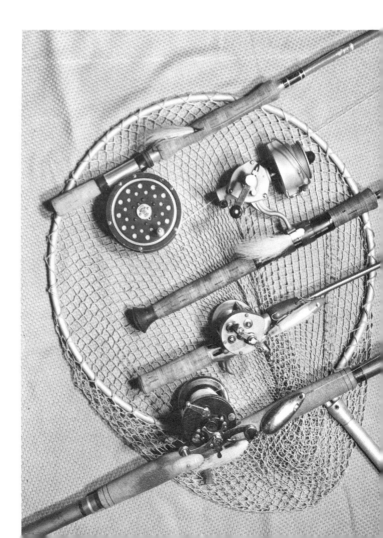

The point to be stressed is the current agreement that every tackle combination, from ultra-light on up, has a definite niche and a limited sphere of greatest efficiency in a modern striped bass sport fishery. As a result, today's ardent bassers tote a variety of outfits.

It is likely that the boom in spinning deserves maximum credit for a palace revolution in strategy and technique. Fly casting and baitcasting initially led the lightweight approach, yet neither advanced so rapidly as fixed-spool gear after that European system had invaded our shores and posted signal victories over time-honored, revolving-spool combinations. The last named is still called "conventional," although on a coastal scale one must wonder whether the nomenclature has not become obsolete.

In spite of the fact that spinning was first received in the United States with hearty skepticism and verbal abuse—the striper fishing regulars of early post-war years referred to fixed-spool reels as "coffee grinders" or "foreign devils" and to the entire combination as "yo-yo tackle"—spinning proved a major factor in the development of sport fishing. There are several reasons why this happened, all of them beneficial.

Basically, fixed-spool is best suited to light casting and far inferior to revolving-spool for certain tasks such as trolling, heavy surf work, or accurate baitcasting. There is no way that the technique can challenge fly-rodding in the presentation of tiny feather lures, a burgeoning game worth discussion in another chapter.

However, spinning was first publicized as a cure-all for beginners who were baffled by the revolving-spool's requirement of an educated thumb. It is far easier to master basic spinning when attempting to throw out a bait or lure into the blue and to retrieve the tempter *sans* backlash. In spite of fixed-spool's "line slough," which is backlash by another name, and in spite of the line-twisting usually resulting from reeling frantically while line is pouring off the spool under a pre-set drag, the whole *schmeer* was—and is—easier to get acquainted with than the conventional one which originated in America's southern heartland as a tool with which to subdue inland black bass.

Quite naturally, early exponents of the art, often the rankest of amateurs in advanced sport fishing, joined together in a cult that proclaimed its new discipline superior to all other. Certainly no cure-all, the technique served a purpose never envisioned by hyped-up beginners on the striper coasts. Fixed-spool gear brought millions of tyro anglers to the sea and to inland waters, where they swiftly learned the facts of life.

Gradually, these incoming boys and girls, while still learning the intricacies of their chosen tackle, made the (to them) astonishing discovery that other techniques were not outmoded after all! Having been bloodied by a sort of boot-camp training, many determined to master the revolving-spool and fly casting. Now that they were thoroughly hooked and eager to learn, it was no longer a time of reluctance or fear. Each had gained a measure of knowledge and had to conclude, logically, that other disciplines were equally specialized and worth learning.

As a result, modern striped bass fishermen investigate all of the techniques and tackle combinations. This does not dismay tackle manufacturers and, best of all, it ensures greater success for the angler. Spinning gains in popularity, and rightly so. Perhaps it starts with ultra-light, which can be either a journey into frustration or a calculated and highly professional approach keyed to a correct and subtle balance of rod, reel, and line, plus the tiniest of lures.

We watched, fascinated, on one bright blue morning when school bass were rushing bait in the suds. A half-dozen youngsters armed with light, one-handed spinning rods (rated about ten-pound test) caught striper after striper. A single adult die-hard, armed with a big surf outfit, went entirely hungry. Although an expert, he simply could not compete with the kids because it was impossible for him to present miniature jigs or work them seductively. It was a time and a place for delicacy rather than clout.

An aspirant for IGFA honors, if he has learned a trade and is versatile, if he has a forgiving rod and a miniature reel filled with gossamer monofilament and blessed with a smooth drag system, can go well below ten-pound test and succeed. Usually though, excepting those occasions when school bass are readily available and anxious to grab small lures under goldfish bowl conditions, a one-handed spinning rod and well-designed reel filled with ten-pound-test line is far from overpowering.

One afternoon, admiring his prowess, we saw Ray Calabrese of Framingham, Massachusetts, play and land a 45-pound striper on this combination. Of course he was fishing from a boat, which afforded some advantage, but it was a spectacle to be imprinted on memory. A one-handed spinning stick calibrated to handle lures in the one-quarter- to one-ounce bracket is not formidable artillery; it takes skill to prevent break-off after the hook is set.

The one-handed spinning rod generally used, although there are many variations, is a type we designed for bonefishing on the Florida Keys and was first built by the late Amelio DeStefano of Boston. It proved equally versatile for light-tackle striped bass fishing and was soon widely copied. Length ranges from 6½ to 7 feet from butt to tip top. Manufactured in one piece, although two-piece rods will fare equally well, the stick is calibrated to handle lures ranging from one-quarter to one ounce. Below or above that weight bracket, it labors in casting.

Early spinning reels were delicate, prone to malfunction, possessed of primitive, jerky drag systems and forever-snapping bail springs; they have been vastly improved in all size ranges. Almost all of the premier grade models feature somewhat faster retrieve ratios than revolving-spool gear, hence they can be definite aids when a lure must be brought back at flank speed to ensure proper action. In heavy surf casting, the manually operated bail is preferred, and it does not take long to master.

Curiously, although Americans have always favored right-hand drive, hidebound stars-and-stripes people quickly adjust to left-hand cranking. Right-hand or interchangeable drive is readily available. Australians seem to dote on the right-hand handle operation; otherwise, it's 90 percent southpaw. They don't catch striped bass in Australia, but the game is the same.

Spinning rods feature large ring guides, the better to funnel spiraling line pouring off a spool, and these are graduated from a very large gathering ring down to a small and rifled tip top. As is usual with most fishing sticks in casting and the playing of a trophy, five to six guides are used to distribute stress in casting and to prevent the line from slapping while playing the quarry.

Baitcasting, as aforementioned, came out of America's southland where the outfit was specifically designed to take inland black bass. Every quadruple multiplying reel is a descendant of the ancient Kentucky Meeks, which were built like fine watches—but nonetheless have become collector's items far inferior in efficiency to today's precisely balanced products featuring free-spool and smooth star drags. Level-wind worm gears remain popular, although a lot of professionals discard them at once in order to gain an additional few yards of distance. Once mastered, the educated thumb is a keen tool in the smooth laying of line.

Conventional reels and baitcasting rods quickly migrated to salt water, probably first in the Gulf of Mexico where sport fishermen found them ideal in the conquest of seatrout, redfish, and baby tarpon, then northward to the striper coasts. There is a strong return to the system today, thanks to the pinpoint accuracy it achieves and its control of pugnacious fishes after hookup. The package is perhaps at its best in working sheltered waters, such

This chart illustrates a simple method of determining location and spacing of rod guides on a blank.

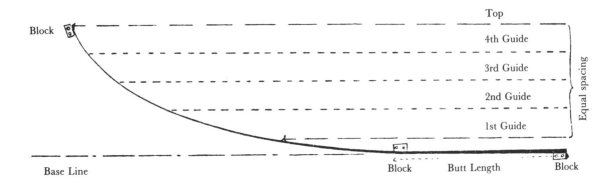

A heavy fly rod can be a potent weapon on stripers feeding in the wash at dawn or dusk.

as sodbank areas where a lure must be dropped precisely on target, often inches away from clutching weeds and brush, or into a miniature pocket surrounded by snags.

Rods tend to be somewhat longer than those prescribed for inland angling, but not by much—say 6 to 7 feet overall. They are almost entirely tubular fiberglass, graphite, or the new boron mix, and there are other subtle differences in the marine variation. Salty anglers like a reasonably fast and limber tip with lots of power amidships.

Reels have not changed very radically, the major differences being a phase-out of the direct drive and the pre-set cub handle, which were efficient in their time, but hardly comparable to smoothly functioning and easily adjusted star drag systems. Free-spool and anti-reverse locks are further refinements. None of the ancient classics, in spite of their beauty and intricate craftsmanship, can begin to compete with this day's advanced designs.

Surf casting, once opined—and still thought to be—a classic method in striped bass fishing, has also undergone a sea change. While noting that one can use any tackle on the beach, and further to repeat that all are efficient under specific conditions, the true high surf outfit has always been a powerful throwing combination and never an ultimate fish-fighting tool. The idea is to get a bait or lure out well beyond the inshore breakers, then to keep running line above furious whitecaps and spume. When big striped bass rush bait at the 200- to 300-foot mark, a long and powerful rod is necessary to place plug or jig right on target.

Length generally ranges from 9 to 11 feet in conventional, often up to 14 in spinning rods. Shorter sticks are favored by jetty jockeys, or for casting from the decks of boats where it becomes difficult to wind up and throw. Butt length is then diminished, measuring anywhere from 18 to 20 inches.

Even in the high surf, too much rod can be a mistake. Modern tournament casters feel that anything over 11 feet handicaps, rather than benefits, an average-sized human being. This limitation of length applies to heavy spinning as well as to conventional heaving. In competition, and assuming that line tests and terminal weights are roughly similar, conventional always out-throws fixed-spool gear. Many find this hard to believe, yet record books prove it so.

There are certain benefits in heavy spinning, for limber tips and power at mid-section enable anglers to toss lightweight lures more efficiently than would be possible with conventional sticks calibrated to, say, the three- to five-ounce weight bracket. Fixed-spool cannot compete when these heavier offerings are used, but they are right on the mark with light stuff. Most over-the-counter rods are fitted with five to six graduated ring guides in order to distribute stresses. Both spinning and conventional rods have long butts which aid a two-handed technique that is simply a step up from the one-handed rod that does well at close range.

Reels are, for the most part, rugged open-faced spinning types or wide-spooled conventionals. In Australia, North Africa and to a certain extent along the Pacific Coast of the United States, the tough and efficient side-cast Alvey pleases surf casters. Those who favor conventional reels have little patience with level-wind devices, since breaking waves too often are laden with particles of sand. If this grit infiltrates an exposed and delicate worm gear you are out of business pending on-site cleaning. Suspended sand is less likely to invade gearing shielded by side plates, yet quick take-down is a desired feature in the event that flushing with clean sea water or use of a grease-cutting solvent becomes necessary.

Any fine surf casting reel should be light, strong, free-spooling, fitted with a smoothly functioning drag and an anti-reverse lock. At one time American striper fishermen liked a rather narrow-spooled conventional reel. It is worth noting that most of Europe's tournament casters have proved that this type achieves greatest distance. However, the choice in this country, for everyday angling, is the somewhat easier-to-control wide spool. For the most flawless operation, the spool is made of tough, hard plastic or one of the light metal alloys that help to defeat backlash caused by an overdose of centrifugal force. Line capacity in standard bass fishing should be at least 200 yards.

Quick take-apart design and built-in reel clamps fitted with butterfly nuts are features to look for, although they will not add to or detract from casting potential. Gear ratio of 3½ to 1 has long been deemed suitable in revolving spool, yet if a faster retrieve is essential, one may easily locate models featuring a 5 to 1 ratio, a definite aid in working some tinclads and bucktail jigs.

Anti-backlash devices of different types help to defeat that ancient bird's nest wryly called an "overrun" by folk who cannot bear to admit error. These range from the judicious use of oil in bearings to counter-balances to the old and excellent Penn Squidder's fins on the inside of the spool's bell. The latest models of throwing reels are cleverly designed to defeat backlash while ensuring maximum distance in a cast. Within the memory of middle-aged bassmen, most of the devices exacted a price. That is no longer true.

Of course the hallmark of an enthusiastic conventional surf caster is the groove in his left thumb, carved there by guiding tight line to flawless level on a reel's spool. This dexterity is learned gradually until it becomes almost instinctive. Thumb pressure is hard at the start of the cast, then is released while the spool is gently feathered to sense the first indication of a building loop, the first indication of a backlash. We as individuals illustrate the two schools of thought in such casting. Lyman keeps his thumb at the edge of the spool from start to finish; Woolner puts pressure on the spool's center at the start of the cast, then may shift to the edge. Both are right as far as their individual styles are concerned.

Spin casters similarly guard against trouble with an index finger caressing the running mono as it spirals out behind a thrown lure. They do not acquire the livid groove on a left thumb, but a right index finger can get mighty sore if—without some sort of a finger stall—they essay the snap casting of heavy artificials.

Trolling gear is a new dimension. One can troll with just about any given outfit, including spinning or fly casting tackle, but for various good and true reasons revolving-spool gear fares best. There are exceptions; for example, on school to medium-sized bass in a tidal estuary or other reasonably quiet and sheltered waters, a heavy fly rod, a large single-action reel filled with monofilament and tipped with a streamed sea worm, spinner and worm, or just a light wobbler can work wonders. This is a stealthy, slow-speed operation, once relying strictly on an ash breeze, yet a small and quiet electric or outboard motor seems to pose no handicap. You will want a little shallow-draft boat that will not sustain injury when an occasional pile of rocks is brushed in passing.

On offshore grounds, unless line-test records are sought, tackle is beefed up to a certain extent. Rods are still synthetic, either tubular or solid. A 30-pound test rating will handle the largest striper in existence, yet there are occasions when more clout is needed, as in wire-lining with heavy lures.

Boat sticks are short, seldom exceeding 7 feet in length from an 18-inch butt to tip top, which really makes them better fighting tools. Roller guides are an advantage always and, at the very least, the tip top should be a roller type. In striped bass fishing there is little need for a gimbal nock, although a belt socket harness may prove pleasant in the event of a long battle with a big bass. We have never found either necessary, nor is it likely that you will be in the playing and boating of a new world's record. Stick a rubber cap on the end of the stick and let it go at that. At least you will not jab yourself in some tender southern extremity of the anatomy.

Hefty trolling combinations are used when big rips and surging tidal currents appreciably aid the quarry, and in wire-line fishing for other reasons which will shortly be discussed. The use of wire is comparatively new, growing in popularity because it is both sporting and ethical when properly employed.

Depending upon a given task, revolving-spool reels may range from miniatures on up to approximately 4/0; no larger is ever necessary for striped bass under any fishing condition. Smoothly functioning drag systems, either star or lever, are essential. On larger models gearing will usually be 2½ to 1, often upward of that in smaller versions that are intended to serve many purposes. On the lightest of trolling winches and the so-called bay reels, level-wind is practical for the neat laying of line. Some old reprobates will not select this option, but it is an advantage.

Among the family of salt water reels there is an extremely narrow-spooled version which actually looks something like a herculean single-action fly casting winch. It is not. It is singularly adapted to wire-line use and we will talk about it in a following chapter.

Aside from the packaging of Christmas presents, lashing rigged eels, and otherwise accomplishing plebian mule-work, twisted linen Cuttyhunk line is no longer of consequence to any advanced angler, certainly not as a fishing line. Nylon and dacron multifilaments and, of course, nylon monofilament have entirely won center stage. Fly lines are a separate breed of cats, yet they also go the synthetic road to nearly complete supremacy in presenting fur, feathers, and hair.

Nylon edged into the game very early and was quickly followed by dacron. In the beginning, neither was very impressive. Monofilament was excessively elastic and unstable, while dacron braids were rough enough to be called "hot lines" by surf casters. Blisters on right thumbs and livid grooves on the left were grouchily accepted as inevitable. Within a couple of decades these problems were largely corrected.

In passing, it is worth recalling that the once-popular linen twist called

Cuttyhunk was no gentle strand: It would practically melt a right thumb if distance throwing was attempted prior to a few short wetting heaves. The line was abrasive and it gave the angler a shower bath each time he whipped a tin squid toward the horizon. Still, Cuttyhunk was good string for its time and it was stronger when wet than dry.

Nylon and dacron multifilaments and nylon monofilament have just about defeated all of the organics. Mono is increasingly favored by striper addicts for use with all the tackle combinations. Single-strand line is good, inexpensive, and fairly easy on the thumb, although an angler can still raise a blister if he does not make a couple of short throws to "lubricate" the string with water before trying to lay out a long cast.

Mono is available in a variety of colors ranging from a preferably translucent mist-grey through the entire spectrum to vividly fluorescent blue, yellow, and orange. Stripers seem to favor no one over another and champions of activated string gain something of an edge by knowing precisely where their lures are at any given time. This is a distinct advantage when two or more lines are trolled, since the visible spread can be better controlled to prevent tangling.

Bulk mono is widely employed, although it is not the quality-controlled product offered by major companies at a slightly greater price. Quite often, unless labeled "IGFA-rated," stated tests are somewhat deceptive—and it works both ways. Firms have been known to boast of the, say, "strongest 15-pound-test mono in the world"; it sure is—since it pulls a checking scale to 17 or 18!

Bulk spools are haphazardly rated. When Rosa Webb posted her all-tackle world woman's record on striped bass (64½ pounds), her line was lighter than she thought it was. Supposedly 40-pound test, on IGFA's testing machines the sample parted at a little under 30 pounds. IGFA-rated lines are purposely built to break at an ounce or so under a stated test. This slight margin for error prevents frustration when judges examine tackle used in applying for record.

Striped bass are not sabre-toothed tigers: Their mouths feel like medium sandpaper, yet there is rarely need to use a wire leader. Monofilament invariably gets the nod, with tests somewhat heavier than the running line. In most casting or trolling, leader length is fairly short, ranging from 12 to 18 inches in light spinning, to perhaps a yard with heftier gear. Surf casters who employ light lines increasingly copper their bets by using a shock leader long enough to provide sufficient overhang at the beginning of the cast and extend back to three or four turns around the reel's spool. The object is to prevent break-off during the initial stress of a hard cast. Thus, using an 11-foot surf rod as an example, the "shocker" will be 13 to 15 feet long.

Connections are vitally important, especially where light tackle is used. We do not intend to list all of the knots used, for the simple reason that this information is readily available in a host of other books and pamphlets distributed by line-makers. One of the most comprehensive studies is *Practical Fishing Knots*, a work co-authored by Lefty Kreh and Mark Sosin.

Excepting occasions where ounces really count in light tackling striped bass, an angler is rarely handicapped if he practices tying a few. The Improved Clinch terminal connection is most popular because it requires little dexterity and is efficient, if not quite up to a dubious 100 percent factor credited to other knots. One should employ the Palomar Knot where it is feasible; this one *is* a fraction stronger than Improved Clinch, easily constructed, neat, and highly effective.

Our feeling is that double lines are best secured with the Spider Hitch, a connection easily mastered and one that boasts strength almost identical to that of the much-publicized Bimini Twist. The major difference is the fact that a Hitch can be completed very swiftly by a single person, while the Twist requires more time and has been described (only somewhat unfairly) as the knot requiring two dexterous men and a fence post to construct. Either connection is close to ultimate, being both very close to the 100 percent strength factor.

In striped bass fishing, indeed in almost all salt water angling, *keep terminal hardware to an absolute minimum.* There will be a need for barrel swivels (the ball-bearing types are most efficient) and for locking snaps. Do not invest in the old, angular safety-pin snap, since it often opens under pressure. There is a need for some use of bright colored glass or plastic beads in trolling or bait fishing, plus a judicious use of "doodlebug floats" for a bottom-fished offering a foot or so off the sea bed to avoid crabs and other deep-down scavengers.

Now you are armed for combat with striped bass, yet hardly a master of the art. One must think about proper use of baits and artificial lures, how to "read the water," how to take advantages of specific tides and tidal currents, perhaps how to think like a fish. Did you really think this campaign would be a piece of cake?

5 · Natural Smorgasbord

NATURAL BAIT IN WHICH A HOOK IS IMBEDDED makes one of the oldest devices in the world for taking salt water fish. Actually, only the net and the spear can claim greater antiquity—and who wants to dabble in Stone Age sport? Despite the ancient history of the baited hook, it is still highly effective and can be particularly successful when the quarry is a striped bass.

A striper will eat just about anything that does not eat it first! Bass may even make newspaper headlines by gulping down such rare viands as an unfortunate tern, a stray end of frankfurter, or a cigar butt. Usually, however, best results are enjoyed by the angler who is concerned about careful preparation and presentation of bona fide forage, by the keen student of camouflage who strives to defeat suspicion by keeping lines and terminal hardware inconspicuous. No sportsman should be troubled by a lack of promising tempters and each is best offered friskily alive or very freshly dead.

Colleagues who combine the fine arts of angling and criticism will politely lift their eyebrows. Forage *is* abundant and bass *do* have catholic appetites, yet there are stray flies in the amber. Often no more than one or two bait species will be in immediate residence and, too confoundedly often, unpredictable stripers become maddeningly selective. Advising presentation in a natural manner ruffles no feathers, but our exhortation to use live or fresh dead bait will trigger scattered Bronx cheers. A rigged eel, for example, seems to get better and better as its carcass gets worse and worse. Bass, for some reason known only to bass, occasionally develop a cultivated taste for sea worms and clams that are not only dead, but have deteriorated to a point of near-liquefaction.

In defense, we can only cite Standard Operational Procedure—with the proviso that S.O.P. cannot afford to ignore exceptions. Therefore, having separately and together fished every American striper coast, it is our intention to examine the baits most likely to tempt bass, how said winners are normally presented, and finally, how it is sometimes profitable to bend accepted rules.

To the ill-informed, fishing with natural bait is a singularly boring technique pursued by amateurs who employ heavy, crude tackle, and spend much time sitting on their well-padded butts waiting for some marine scavenger to grab a hunk of offal affixed to a grapnel and anchored by a large glob of lead. These unfortunates also believe that the Huck Finn boys with bent pins and birch poles harvest more fish than advanced anglers.

That is just as well, since those of us who adore striped bass utter sighs of relief when we are not crowded out of our hot spots by inept gaggles of ham-handed beginners. Why strive to explain that expertise in the use of natural baits is just as hard-earned a skill as that of casting artificial lures or the precise mechanics of trolling?

Like every specialist, the bait man experiments, but there are certain basics such as proper selection of hooks and, where needed, sinkers. First, because it is one of the most important components in fishing tackle, study hook size, quality, and design. There should be no weakest link in a weapons system, yet lots of otherwise intelligent anglers neglect the one article that *must* perform its duties flawlessly. A hook often fails because it is not sharp, and make a mental note of the fact that few are needle-pointed when purchased. Each should be touched up prior to use and regularly honed thereafter.

The most effective hooks used in striped bass fishing cost only pennies more than those stamped out of inferior metals and peddled by cut-rate outlets. Place greatest trust in name-brand cadmium- or tin-plated steel and stainless steel, both of which are tough and rust-resistant, although the former will suffer corrosion after the plating is worn off by abrasion or constant sharpening. Have nothing to do with thin-wire Japanned types commonly used by fresh water anglers, for these are short-lived in salt and grievously rust-prone. Z-Nickel, no longer favored but still found in a few tackle shops, is a poor choice: The wire is unacceptably heavy and its point blunts easily. Some craftsmen like gold-plated steel in the smaller-sized hooks, and these work well, perhaps adding a smidgeon of come-hither glitter where bend and point are exposed. Go tough, not tender, in selecting a hook. Bass are powerful and they possess strong crushing jaws, so it is usually best to rely on 2-X or 3-X strength ratings.

Ninety percent of the time one will find the single hook most effective, but small trebles may have an edge in the live-lining of certain bait fishes such as mackerel and menhaden. Effective patterns are legion, although a striper enthusiast is apt to get along with three types: These are the O'Shaughnessy, Claw, and Siwash. It is likely that the first named is most popular, yet it is increasingly replaced in the affections of bait jockeys by the Claw or Beak, now generally referred to as the Eagle Claw, which is the Wright & McGill trade name. Siwash, or Pacific Salmon, finds greatest acceptance among the ranks of those who live-line free-swimming tempters. Each style boasts mild debits, and each is magnificently adapted to do certain things well.

O'Shaughnessy, an all-round workhorse, is not kirbed or offset. It is a strong pattern boasting adequate gap and medium-length point, and it can be had in long or short shank, the latter usually chosen where it is deemed wise to conceal all of the hook inside the bait. Siwash's long, slim and tapered point is easier to drive home and also defeats a percentage of cartwheeling, acrobatic stripers. This needle point is both advantage and disadvantage, a good holder but prone to blunting if on-site maintenance is neglected. Like the O'Shaughnessy, Pacific Salmon hooks are rarely kirbed, although it should be noted that a few anglers prefer this configuration, which surely aids solid hooking, and therefore offset the bend with handy pliers. They argue that kirbing destroys balance, which may be important in live-lining where a fisherman wants his bait to swim as naturally as possible.

Generally, the Claw is superior to O'Shaughnessy and Siwash in bait fishing. Its needle-sharp point is rolled under to a degree, much like the ancient and highly efficient Hawaiian (O'io) bonefish bend, but never so radically, and it is offset. Models are available with scored barbs on shanks for holding, say, a slithery sea worm in proper position. The type is well chosen for use with any bait other than live-lined. Even there it works, and it works well.

Bait-holder barbs are relatively new, but fishermen have long stopped slippage by lashing or soldering a common pin at the eye of the hook. These do help, although we always have managed to stick the bait-holding pins in our fingers as frequently as we have stuck them through the sacrificial worm's head. A scored shank may also abuse human digits if one becomes careless while stripping off a tired bait.

One somewhat specialized hook type is that used with a small marine sculpin, called a "bullhead" by Pacific Coast bass fishermen. This one is a true double hook and is positioned so that the barbs are presented at and under the sculpin's head, rather than at its tail, and lashed fast with a couple of leader turns aft. The hook is far from heavy-duty, and it is bronzed. With it, plus an accommodating trio of bullheads, we managed to boat three respectable bass during a morning's sortie at China Camp on San Francisco's vast delta impoundment. Anglers also use single 6/0 hooks to saddle bullhead baits in much the same manner.

Do not delude yourself into thinking that a larger-than-normal hook will prove more effective than standard sizes and strengths. We learned this through experience while swimming rigged eels on a famous North Atlantic ground. Standard rigging was then—and still is in areas where large "snakes" are strung with three singles—an 8/0 O'Shaughnessy at the head, a 7/0 amidships, and a 6/0 tail-end Charley, each fastidiously sharpened. The arrangement usually works like grease, but one night stripers unaccountably

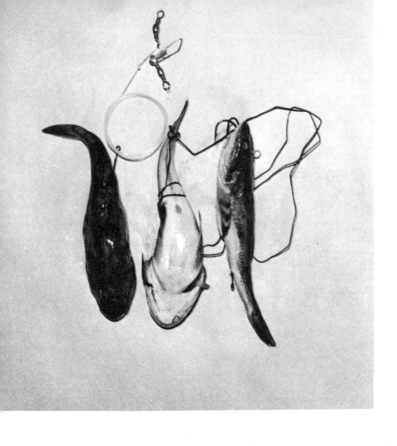

These sculpins, called bullheads *by Pacific Coast anglers, are rigged for use.*

straightened all the hooks. After sun-up, scowling over black coffee, we rigged a couple of eels with stout 10/0 Sobeys. *Let's see the cusses bend these!*

They did not bend the new meat hooks: They just spat out every one after striking hard. Although each point was triangulated to an edge that would grab a careless passer-by, there was too rapid a taper and the confounded things would not penetrate. Our sorrowful conclusion was that big Sobey or Martu hooks are fine for the harvesting of blue marlin and tuna, but not bass.

It is likely that nobody needs anything larger than an 8/0 hook to stick and land the largest striper in existence, and less clout often suffices. Pacific anglers experience no difficulties with hooks far smaller than those favored in the East and even may post higher success ratios. Atlantic regulars shrug their shoulders and make the blanket statement that western bait species run smaller than those roaming the suds from New England to Hatteras.

In any event, acquire a selection of long- and short-shanked singles ranging from 1/0 to possibly 9/0, plus a few in the #2 to #4 range for ultra-light work where miniature baits, such as shrimp or killifish, will be presented. Trebles for bait fishing seldom need be larger than 4/0. Fit the punishment to the crime.

Other than in highly specialized work a striper fisherman need carry only a few sinker designs in different weights, depending on depths and current strengths. On soft bottoms such as sand, clay, or mud, the pyramidal shape is popular because it digs and holds. The dipsey and its close cousin, the bank sinker, provide satisfaction on rocky or rubbled bottoms where angular weights are more apt to hang up. There are uses for the pierced egg and, especially with light tackle, split shot in both BB and buckshot sizes. Rubber-cored clinch-ons are worthy where weight will be held to a minimum.

Trollers are best served by streamlined, cigar-shaped models boasting molded-in swivels and, sometimes, snaps. Keeled trolling sinkers work well and help to prevent line twist where the whole bait or a strip is dragged aft. Dipsey and egg sinkers share a place in deep trolling, as does the aptly named cannonball weight on a quick-release swivel. (This last is a Pacific Coast choice and has never been adopted on the eastern seaboard.)

Choosing the proper weight, after determining the correct design, for a given task is of major importance. Use the lightest sinker that will hold bottom or otherwise do its intended work. This naturally will in part be governed by the tackle employed and by the forces brought to bear by current and wave action. In baiting a high and turbulent surf, pyramids or dipseys in the two- to four-ounce range, with a few even heavier, are standards. Most spin casters choose the lesser weights, while masters of big conventional surf outfits go the opposite route. Ultra-light enthusiasts prefer much less bulk and use pierced eggs, clamp-ons, split shot, or junior grade dipseys and pyramids.

Angling literature bulges with step-by-step diagrams of terminal rigs, all well chosen under certain conditions, but not all essential to a bassing man. That worthy may do very well with a minimal selection assembled on the grounds or purchased from a handy tackle shop. Most commonly employed is the fishfinder arrangement, which is simply an eyed swivel with a pendant snap to attach a sinker. This small and inexpensive article is slipped over running line. A swivel tied to the butt end of the leader acts as a stop and therefore, in theory, a striper can pick up a bait and move off without feeling drag created by an anchoring weight. Various regulars are unconvinced, opining that drag will always be there because of line tension and current flow.

Therefore doubters catch bass with the simplest rig of all—a baited hook with a sinker firmly attached to a dropper loop some 20 to 30 inches ahead of an offering or by a three-way swivel. Variations, used with a fishfinder as well as a static sinker, include the use of more than one hook—two or even three equally spaced on droppers. Where twin barbs are used, the terminal hardware is called a hi-low rig.

Popular among striped bass fishermen of the metropolitan New York–New Jersey seaboard is the "doodlebug," which utilizes one or more floats positioned ahead of the sinker and designed to buoy up a bait over the heads of bottom-feeding scavengers. These floats, which may be small, clear plastic bubbles or spheres, or barrel shapes of cork, are often painted bright red, yellow, or a combination of the two colors. Sometimes a few glass or plastic beads are attached to add greater attraction. A number of doodlebugs are armed with hooks and dressed with hair or feathers so that they look much

Seaworms and "Jersey doodlebugs" float rigs are used to keep bait just above bottom-feeding scavengers.

like a fly-rod popping bug. A sweetener of worm or a strip of squid may help. The technique prevents frustration when the bottom seems paved with crabs, sea robins, skates, or other garbage collectors. No matter what the arrangement, rely on essentials and forego bulky snaps, chains, leather thongs, and more swivels than are necessary. Keep the rig simple and practical, stripped of excess baggage.

Often no weight is used in live-lining a bait that is expected to swim naturally. In that case, the chosen tempter is kept in an aerated well until harnessed for its trip. Small-craft operators make do with a plastic trash can for the live-well, which is aerated by periodically bailing and re-filling with oxygenated sea water, or by a container suspended over the transom, sometimes troublesome because it hampers cruising from one location to another. A deck-mounted, battery-aerated well is always most satisfactory.

Once in action, one may succeed with either spinning or revolving-spool tackle, the latter being undoubtedly the most efficient. Monofilament line invariably gets the nod, with average strength ranging from 20- to 30-pound test. There are subtle variations in technique.

Where medium-sized bait such as mackerel, menhaden, or herring are much used, hooking arrangements may include a single 6/0 to 8/0 barb inserted through the skin just ahead of the dorsal fin. However, a percentage of anglers like a stinger pinned close to the caudal peduncle. In recent years sportsmen have displayed great faith in the use of a treble hook, maintaining that it prevents loss of the quarry when a single barb manages to twist and bury itself in the relatively hard flesh of a bait. Placement depends on individual preference. One prong of a 3/0 to 4/0 treble may be stuck lightly through the skin of the bait's back, yet many prefer driving it through the roof of, say, a menhaden's mouth to protrude through its hard nose. On many occasions where a treble is used, the fisherman strikes his bass immediately after it takes a bait. Usually, though, where a single hook is favored, free-spooling seems to work best until the quarry pauses to turn and swallow its meal.

There should be no doubt when a strike is occurring in live-lining, for a lively bait flutters wildly and moves with short bursts of speed when pursued. Often this is a near-surface action accompanied by a good deal of spouting white water. The challenge is to master one's excitement and to prevent outgoing line from backlashing. That is done by keeping an educated thumb on a revolving spool's reel until it is time to flip a clutch and strike back, or by lightly palming the face of a spinning reel before engaging bail and drag.

On occasion a float makes sense in live-lining. This can be a bright-colored penny balloon or a pegged sphere made of cork or Styrofoam. It

The two best methods of hooking live menhaden for use on striped bass.

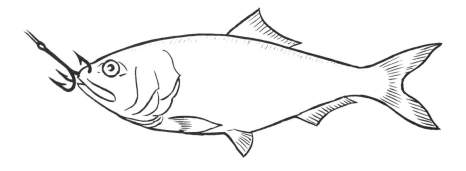

ensures that a bait cannot dive into the bottom jungles, as eels invariably do when allowed a measure of freedom. This type of vertical positioning also works the other way, usually with a bait fish and a sinker suited to bottom conformation: unless the bait is a natural lover of bottom tangles, it will swim in the current a leader's length above the anchoring weight. This trick works well with alewives, menhaden, and the Pacific Coast's shiner perch, an excellent striper bait which produces whether anchored or deep-drifted.

Deep-drifting can be a combination of live-lining and restraint. The rig on which Bob Rocchetta took his 76-pound all-tackle prizewinner at Montauk consisted of a long leader and a three-way swivel to which was attached a bank sinker. Bob was slow-drifting a live eel when his trophy latched on.

Whatever the natural bait, a nicely built chum slick can bring bass into angling range and sharpen their hunger. At the turn of this century live-liners and surf casters regularly baited grounds with minced lobster, herring, menhaden, and other delicacies. Grass shrimp ensured a great many bragging catches, and still do so, although the technique is in partial eclipse. Tiny grass shrimp, "stretched" with uncooked rolled oats to the ratio of a box of oats to a quart of shrimp, make an almost irresistible chum. Hooked bait may be several of the transparent midgets threaded on a single hook, other natural tempters, or artificial lures. Nobody is about to use lobsters in a modern slick, but present-day mixtures are not expensive to buy or to prepare with the help of a kitchen meat grinder.

Marine biologists list a surprising number of forage species upon which stripers feast habitually or occasionally. Every classic ground boasts favorites, including a host of small- to medium-sized finfishes. Western bassers consider the Pacific sardine, cut or whole, hard to beat. Anchovies and surf smelt are equally well thought of, as are the shiner perch and bullhead. East, west, or wherever stripers cruise, fish baits are used whole, chunked, or filleted. The head of a mullet, mackerel, or other large specimen can be a pay-off item on bottom. The list of probables is extensive, although one must always consider

The head of a herring, alewife, or other baitfish can be a striper killer, especially during the early spring runs.

the striper's perplexing selectivity. In baiting it's the jam-and-jelly syndrome: As a jovial Swedish immigrant is said to have exclaimed, "Yust when I learn to say *yam*, they change it to *yelly!*"

Without doubt it is necessary to name the American eel a winner, and to note that it is common along the Atlantic Coast, but is never found on Pacific striper grounds. The three largest bass ever listed as all-tackle world's records were taken on this bait. These, in order of succession, were Charles B. Church's legendary 73-pounder, caught off Cuttyhunk, Massachusetts on August 17, 1913; Edward J. Kirker's 72-pounder from the same ground on October 10, 1969; and, lastly as of this writing, Bob Rocchetta's 76-pound trophy boated off Montauk, New York, on July 16, 1981. In addition to these historic fish, eels annually account for thousands of large and small stripers.

Eels are versatile baits—tough, slippery, slimy, effective whether alive or dead, and productive at any size from tiny "shoestrings" on up to those weighty enough to be thrown by a surf caster. Their limber skins are used to adorn artificial lures and eelskin jigs.

It is no trick at all to keep the species alive over a considerable period of time. Hours after they are netted out of a bait shop's holding well, snakes that have been bedded in a mat of salt-wet seaweed and kept reasonably cool may still need a mite of stunning to make them manageable. The affectionate coastal nickname, "snakes," is apt: On dry land an eel looks like a reptile and moves like one. Anglers *have* experimented with the terrestrial garter snake as bass bait, but no stunning successes have been reported. It is likely that the reptile's strong scent is repugnant to a striper, while that of the marine look-alike is pleasant perfume. Pleasant, at any rate, to a bass—even when potent enough in a long-defunct specimen to warp human noses.

Rigged eels are not as widely employed as they were a few decades back, chiefly because there has been a considerable switch to soft plastic substitutes; yet the genuine article does not play second fiddle to an ersatz one. Strung with two or three single hooks, specimens in the 12- to 15-inch bracket are lobbed and retrieved by surf casters, or trolled offshore. Unweighted, these progress only a foot or so beneath the surface. However, it is a simple matter to add or subtract strip lead at the nose to get the desired swimming depth.

Another rigging method is called the eel-bob, in which the eel is strung with a cone-shaped lead slug snugged up forward, in place of the creature's severed head. Wobble-plate-equipped eels have been used for a great many years, the earliest versions utilizing a shaped lead squid, which provided action, plus a built-in forward hook. Later, a little gimmick was constructed from a short length of five-eighths-inch copper tubing hammered to resemble a policeman's whistle and nicknamed—what else—"The Whistle."

Rigging is not difficult, but it takes time and skill. Use a sailmaker's needle or an improvised facsimile made from a length of rigid wire or even a bicycle spoke. Custom needles are available at any tackle shop which caters to

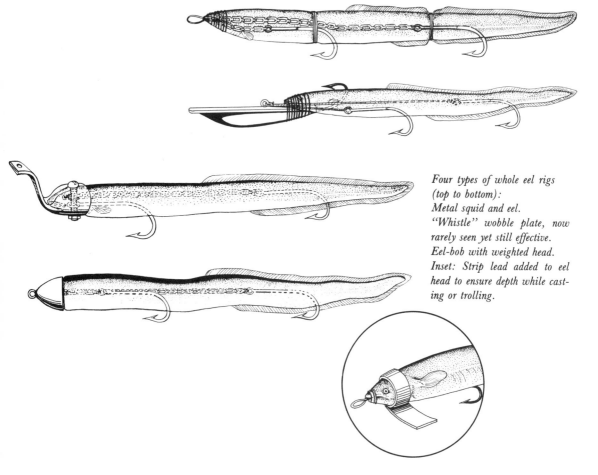

Four types of whole eel rigs (top to bottom):
Metal squid and eel.
"Whistle" wobble plate, now rarely seen yet still effective.
Eel-bob with weighted head.
Inset: Strip lead added to eel head to ensure depth while casting or trolling.

offshore fishing folk. Ideally, this will be made of stainless steel, at least a foot in length, sharply pointed at the business end, and eyed or notched at the other. Heavy nylon monofilament will serve as a hook connector, although you will want a brass or stainless steel "toilet chain" if chopping bluefish haunt the striper grounds. A majority of riggers lash hooks in place with linen line. (Use of a brass chain, incidentally, is not recommended if an eel is to be kept in preserving brine for any length of time, because the resulting electrolysis swiftly destroys steel hooks.)

There is limited use of sharpened tubes to core the backbones out of eels prior to rigging. This guarantees greater flexibility of the offering—perhaps too great, since an over-limber snake regularly fouls when it is cast. Natural color is fine, although "bluing," accomplished by scouring with sand or steel wool, is advocated by a number of beachcombers. All eels, served up dead or alive, catch more bass by night than during daylight hours. When cast from shore or boat, the most effective retrieve is a slow to medium one with a regular up-and-down pulsing of the rod. A living eel will do its own share of sinuous squirming, but it is necessary to pause regularly in winding a rigged

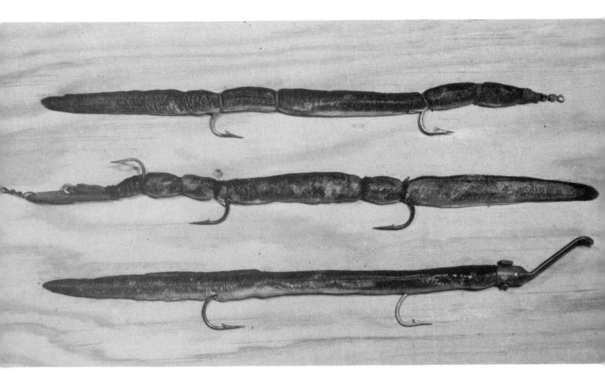

Rigged eels ready for casting or trolling.

Basic eel rigging. The chain-to-stinger-hook model, is most often used when sharp-toothed species, such as bluefish, range the striper grounds.

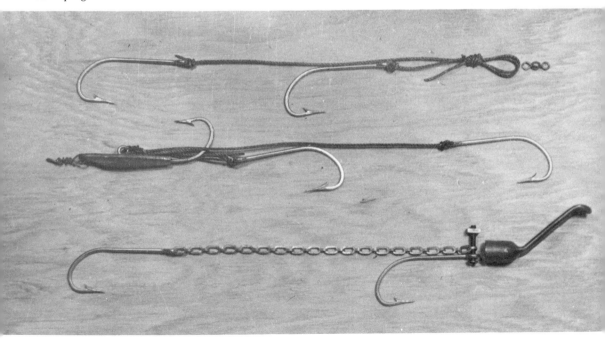

version. Unless equipped with a wobble-plate of some sort, a dead bait exhibits no seductive motion as it is pulled forward. However, as the caster pauses by lowering the rod tip, the snake reacts to the current and wriggles violently. That is why most strikes are registered during this brief dropback.

Live eels can be cast and retrieved quite as effectively as rigged ones and many bassmen hold them superior for catching fish. One hook, usually a single 6/0 or 7/0, is thrust through the lips and out an eye socket. The retrieve is then similar to that with a dead, strung version, but fast enough to prevent the creature from diving and seeking sanctuary on bottom.

Eelskin rigs, really combinations of natural and artificial bait, once saw heavy service, but for some curious reason have declined in popularity. One version of this time-tested killer is a lead-headed jig with a ring secured aft both to attach the skin and to permit water to flow through. Fitted with one or two barbs, the skin is presented much as it is on a standard lead-head bucktail. There is also a trolling type of eelskin rig made of light metal tubing, and early trollers sometimes placed their trust in a yard-long, many-hooked monster appropriately dubbed a Longfellow.

Readily available on most seacoasts, the squid is a jet-propelled cuttlefish esteemed by bass and served up in a number of ways: whole, chunked, or in strips; on bottom, trolled, or cast meager distances. Where a whole squid is trolled, one or two single hooks are rigged through the envelope or body cavity and sewed into position to prevent slippage. Some canny mates employ a single long-shanked barb with a bullet-shaped lead-head at the hook's eye to prevent surfacing and skipping.

Since squid progress tail first, and swiftly, the hook's point emerges at the creature's true head, nestled among trailing tentacles. When "ripe," an otherwise nearly scentless cuttle fish smells even worse than a rotten eel!

Squid—one of the all-time great baits used by striper fishermen.

Fortunately, bass dislike them in that state. One can preserve a squid in strong brine, where it assumes a shocking pink coloration and becomes a poor substitute for the fresh and tempting.

Prepared rigs, usually consisting of two 5/0 to 7/0 single hooks connected by leader wire or monofilament, work well. On site, and depending upon the size of the bait in residence, one can prepare a substitute by linking two or three singles, barb through eye. This contraption casts like a sack of wet sea plums, but can be effective when placed on target. Every now and then anglers will succeed admirably with squid heads presented on bottom.

Among premier bass baits are a variety of marine worms which may be fished from the deepest depths to near the surface—cast, live-lined, or trolled. Almost always these are best offered alive and wriggling, yet there are occasions when stripers will inhale sea worms after they are well on their way to a marine graveyard. Therefore, do not discard obviously defunct squirmers until they are too far gone to remain on the hook, or at least have been given a chance to produce.

Most common of the marine worms favored by anglers are genus *Nereis* or the genus *Glycera*, the former known to anglers variously as sandworms and clamworms, while the latter are called bloodworms or muckworms. Those of the *Nereis* clan have strong nippers at their heads and are reddish-brown to green in color. *Glycera* boast less pronounced nippers, are more red in color, and "bleed" when broken. Both, along with their sisters and their cousins and their aunts—lugworms, pileworms and ribbon worms—will catch bass wherever linesides enjoy hearty meals.

Before we wade into the business of fishing with worms, it should be reported that the squirmers have yet to be raised successfully in any quantity under artificial conditions. This aim may be achieved in a foreseeable future, but all of the bait now used by anglers is either individually harvested or dug up and marketed by commercial operators. In some areas a local license is needed to dig worms.

On fishing grounds one can keep these fine baits alive and healthy in salt-wet seaweed or a commercially prepared bedding. Keep them cool, but never let worms come into contact with fresh water because that will swiftly kill them. If ice is used as a coolant, keep it in the bottom of a horizontally separated container. Regularly pick out worms that have died, or the entire group will swiftly succumb.

Usually worms should stream naturally when attached to a hook, not bunched up. One or two, threaded well up on a shank, fare best in bottom-bouncing, trolling, or live-lining in a current. Push the hook's point into the worm's mouth, slide it up to the barb's eye, and bring the point out through the belly. Now and then a glob of bait will work better than streamed individuals. This is most profitable in bottom fishing, seldom in drifting, never in trolling. A rubber band just behind the worm's head will keep it from sliding down the hook shank.

When surf casting, especially with the exceptionally attractive clam-worm, tempters tend to break off and fly in all directions during a hard snap cast. Veterans therefore lob, applying what might be described as a smoothly accelerated sweep. However, after touchdown in the area thought to be ideal, an angler's artistry is far from completed.

It is most productive to hold a bait rod in your hand, yet periods of inaction often necessitate sand spiking. In that case, particularly in night fishing, one can paper-clip a small streamer of visible white cloth to the line just below the rod's tip top. Some fishermen wrap a few turns of fluorescent plastic tape around the very end of the stick. Both tricks provide warning when a striper nibbles or moves off with a morsel in its mouth.

As in most angling techniques, it is wise to "cover the water." Following a cast, if no strikes are registered, retrieve gently, with frequent pauses, a few yards at a time. In this way, more potential feeding ground is covered. Puffs of sand or mud created by sinker movement serve as attractions in themselves. The trick works with all bottom baits.

While worms are highly effective, shrimp, crabs, clam flesh, sand eels, and a host of other minnows or crustaceans share the hit parade. Technique is roughly similar, but with some modifications. Sand eels, for example, can be used singly, but are often more attractive when several are strung together through the eyes on the point of a single hook. Expect this presentation to succeed when sand eels are plentiful, often littering the beach in wind rows after a high tide. As the flood recedes, many defunct sand eels are swept back to sea. There are then so many of the silvery delicacies in the water that a solitary fishlet seems less than entrancing to a foraging striper intent on scooping up a whole bundle at one whack.

Crabs of various species are also bass killers and some anglers swear by them as *ne plus ultra*. Stripers do hit the mature, hard-shelled beasts, but seem

Mummichogs, called killifish *in many areas, also catch bass.*

Sand eels are effective baits on Atlantic beaches.

Mullet, rigged with and without weight for trolling.

Live mackerel is a popular tempter among live-liners on the Atlantic seaboard.

more addicted to shedders which are soft, leathery in texture, and temporarily lacking armor. Where hard-shelled crab is employed, a single hook is inserted at the edge of the top shell and pushed through the bottom so that the point emerges. Large crabs may profitably be halved or quartered, while smaller creatures are best used whole. Soft-shells, or shedders, will not stay on the hook without some form of lashing, so a barb is not struck into the flesh. Instead, lay your hook across the leathery back and bind it in place with sewing thread or a couple of elastic bands. Old timers used ladies' hairnets for this office.

Crabs can be presented right on bottom with an appropriate sinker and rig, yet are deadliest when drifted on a tidal current. Almost any of the species can be used successfully; on the Atlantic Coast the highly favored—by human gourmets as well as bass—blue crab is a winner. So is the calico crab, often a prime choice of anglers.

Clam flesh is strong medicine at times, and the lowly bivalve always takes a fair share of stripers. A soft-shell or "steamer" may be offered whole and judiciously cracked so that the juices escape. Generally, though, only the flesh is used, pierced as securely as possible and wrapped around the hook. There is one situation in which sea clams, such as the big skimmer and small cherry stone or quahog, seem to be taken in preference to all else in another of those exceptions to the fresh bait rule.

During violent coastal storms, clams are torn from their moorings and dashed ashore on a high-course tide. There the bivalves die swiftly. With the return of fine weather this deteriorating mass is washed seaward, and the bass feast. It then does not matter whether you offer fresh clam or a smelly gob collected right at the high-tide line: You will be in business while colleagues using other tempters, natural or artificial, are talking to themselves and going fishless. Look for the clues—a massive scattering of marooned clams after a blow—and rightly assume that the stage is set for a striper blitz.

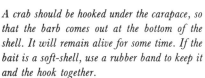

A crab should be hooked under the carapace, so that the barb comes out at the bottom of the shell. It will remain alive for some time. If the bait is a soft-shell, use a rubber band to keep it and the hook together.

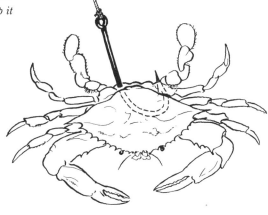

All of the various shrimps please hungry bass and, as previously mentioned, they excel in a chum slick. However, the tasty little kickers are no longer widely used as bait along the North Atlantic seaboard, thanks to the scarcity of the larger types on cold-water grounds and the escalation of price at bait shops. Semi-tropical prawns, available at any supermarket, will do, and the tiny grass shrimp is superb, its sole handicap being its small size. Stripers dote on mantis shrimp, not a true shrimp at all, which grows to ten inches or slightly more. This one, so far as we know, has never been stocked by bait dealers. The best sources are commercial fisheries landings where some may be obtained—if the dragger crewmen like the cut of your jib.

Anglers of our Pacific Coast increasingly use ghost shrimp, a burrower that is spaded or suction-pumped out of mud flats. This tidbit pleases striped bass and, lightly hooked, it brings good news when fished on the bottom or drifted in a brisk current.

While it is hardly recommended as one of the all-time-great temptations, bass have often been caught on what is whimsically described as a "bait cocktail." It is, as the name quaintly implies, a medley of popular hors d'oeuvres, such as a sea worm, a strip of squid, a pinch of shrimp, and a tiny fillet of sand eel. Ingredients depend on the forage species available. Arguments in favor are based on the attraction of the scent wafted into surrounding waters.

A cocktail for bass? It may be worth trying, but still. . . . Any regionally popular natural bait presented in a lifelike manner just has to signal a happy hour for stripers—and for the fishermen who seek them.

6 · A Shoal of Lures

NEVER BEFORE IN THE HISTORY OF STRIPED BASS fishing have anglers been so well equipped with potent artificial lures. A few of these tempters are relatively antique, while others are muscular, well-engineered versions of baits initially designed to catch fresh water fishes. There is no great diversity of basic types, yet variation and improvement is constant, thanks to advanced building materials and manufacturing know-how. So swiftly have artificials moved toward perfection that many of the excellent early creations have been relegated to near obscurity.

When a big striped bass engulfs a lure, no man or woman of ordinary emotions will pause to wonder why. At that climactic moment it is enough to feel the shock of a powerful strike, to groan with pure delight as the fish goes into that characteristic tail-slapping, cartwheeling, or bulldogging fight for freedom. After the fury has subsided, an angler may furrow his salt-rimmed brows and wonder: Why should any game fish, particularly an alert species like the striped bass, mistake an artificial lure for the real thing?

The answer, of course, is that no one knows. Ever since the ancient Egyptians experimented with hackle-dressed flies, anglers have been arguing the point and reaching the same nebulous conclusions. Bass strike artificials because they are hungry, angry, playful, or acting on conditioned reflex while defending territorial rights. Quite possibly they mistake the inedible as a forage species, yet exact replicas of living sea creatures have never proven very effective, while lures that represent no known bait in our world oceans have become killers.

Do not count this as a testimonial for wonderful gadgets that are a cross between a shoehorn and a bicycle pedal. Imaginative anglers are forever creating new teasers but, with few exceptions, the various blood-letting, scent-dispensing, incandescent, battery and gas-operated inventions disappoint their makers and fail to interest the bass.

Examine just two of the many lures favored by surf casters, the metal squid and the plug. Certainly the former, though a classic artificial, does not truly resemble any live bait. No minnow of the sea trails feather- or bucktail-adorned hooks, so the appeal has to be vested in the slithery action, commo-

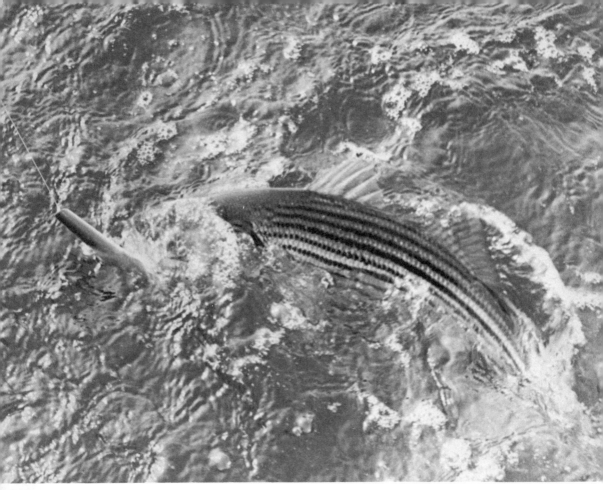

Swirling viciously, a striped bass misses a plug at boatside. Often when they are excited, they strike again and again until hooked.

tion, and flash that roughly simulates a bait fish desperately trying to avoid capture. Surface and sub-surface plugs that thrash, kick, and wiggle do not, for all of their activity, closely match a live tidbit. Possibly a striper does not so much mistake a lure for a natural bait with which it is familiar, as it is fooled into thinking that the thing is simply alive and therefore to be chased, killed and eaten. In choosing a lure, therefore, do not be swayed by exact duplication in form and color of the bona fide article. The acid test boils down to this: *Does it look alive in the water?*

Some of the deadliest of artificials are modern variations of lures invented many years ago. The ancient Polynesians used, and their descendants still use, a trolling jig fashioned of abalone shell and called a "pearl." This lure may well be viewed as a fossil ancestor of the bucktail jig and the trolling spoon. Closer to home, American Indians fashioned wooden plugs fitted with crude hooks. So those we use today are really Johnny-come-latelies, swiftly occupying a niche that was once filled effectively by others' ingenuity.

Lead-head jigs, trolling spoons, tin squids, diamond jigs, and a host of combinations are effective. Soft plastic offerings, including those made of surgical tubing, are much in vogue. Streamer flies and popping bugs come on strong. Updated models of rigged eels, dead or alive, and eelskins catch great numbers of stripers. Since these last are predominantly natural baits, we discuss them in another chapter.

There is no doubt that one of the first popular lures used by American surf casters was the block tin squid, also affectionately called a squid, a tinclad, or simply tin. Never a close copy of natural cuttlefish and more accurately described as a compact casting spoon, tin long served as the beachcomber's primary weapon. Hence striper-oriented surfmen are still nicknamed "squidders," although many have switched their allegiance to plugs.

Thanks to rapid escalation in the price of the metal, today's sand dune fledglings are unlikely to see many of the original block tin squids. Perhaps, as veterans maintain, no other material possesses the soft, almost translucent glow of tin; but aside from relics passed down as heirlooms, or those created by meticulous home craftsmen, for all intents and purposes the real McCoy is gone. For that matter, few of today's well-stocked tackle shops offer the multitude of squid types that graced the shelves when father was a stripling. Many of those now consigned to the shadows of fond memory will return to favor, if only because they have not been bettered.

Leadhead jigs, frequently called bucktails—*though the dressing varies—are deadly striper lures. They require skill in employment.*

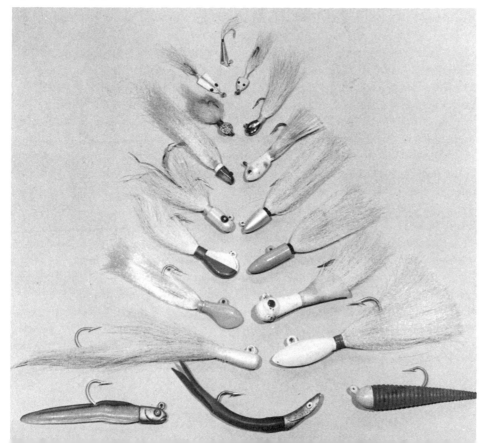

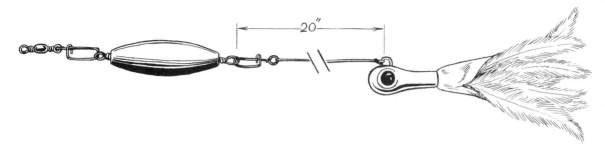

A barrel sinker rigged ahead of a leadhead jig ensures strikes when deep trolling.

During the peak of tinclad popularity in the 1930s and through the thunderous 1940s, these tempters were of roughly three different configurations: the broad, high-riding wobbler, akin to a weighted spoon and designed to match the struggle of deep-bodied bait fish in shoal water or light surf; the keeled squid in many variations, much heavier than the wobbler and job-rated to perform in more turbulent breakers or crashing tide rips; and the slim, rounded, or somewhat flattened and elongated jig intended to simulate a sand eel. These last were bent by hand, but of course all of the casting squids can be, and are, regularly bent, supposedly to improve their action. Fishermen have always considered these artificials best employed in daylight, although there is one notable exception, which we will get to soon.

A fourth general type, which we arbitrarily and maybe erroneously dismiss as a true tinclad, is the diamond jig. That is because it is better suited to vertical jigging at various depths from the cockpit of a fishing boat. That it will catch bass in the suds is quite true. That it is a salty metal lure of tremendous overall importance cannot be denied. But diamonds are most versatile offshore, where they are justifiably ranked high among striper-enticing artificials.

Among the recognized and much appreciated types that every basser once had in his tackle kit are the representatives of the Point Judith Wobbler, the Montauk Keeled Squid, and the Bent Sand Eel. We are not sure which came first, yet it is likely that the simple drail that saw years of service among ancient heave-and-haul handliners must be a contender. Anyhow, the great names out of the recent past are Ferron, Johnston, Belmar, Point Judith, and Sand Eel.

Here it would be easy to stumble into a trap and declare that the deadly specialization that led to a proliferation of squid shapes waned with the passing of classic squidders and the emergence of a new tribe of plug-happy purists, but that is not true. Today's anglers are doing well, thank you, with the immensely popular "hammered knife handle" called Hopkins Lure, with the Acme Kastmaster—really a descendant of the old Eda Splune—and with a selection of Pacific Coast favorites collectively nicknamed "candy bars." All

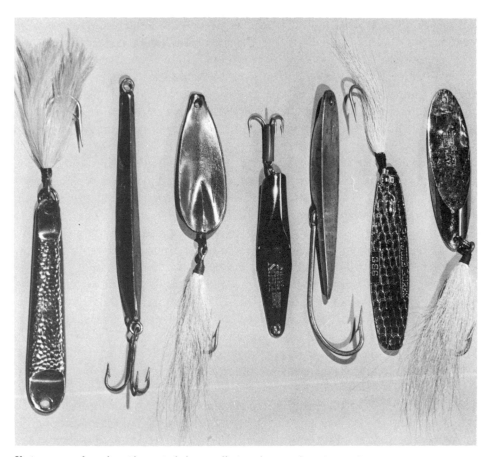

Various types of metal squids, or tinclads, are effective when cast from shore or boat.

of these are offered by more than one manufacturer, which is testimonial to the fact that every successful prototype is almost immediately copied, with slight variations to defeat pending patents by competitors in the field.

Some of the old stand-by models, with the exception of the bent sand eel and the drail, offered superior built-in action. Many of the newcomers, such as Kastmaster, Hopkins, and candy bars are similarly endowed but to a lesser extent, so that clever rod handling and greater speed of retrieve pays off. Spoonlike tins, like the Point Judith Wobbler, are best brought back rather slowly. Speed should be increased when one is working the slimmer keeled jigs, which need a mite more water resistance to induce the illusion of a crippled bait fish dodging through turbulent water. The Johnston Jig, very deep-keeled and compact, unfortunately rarely seen now, is shaped like the hull of a racing sailboat: It is a mighty satisfying squid to throw when an angler must attain maximum range. Kastmasters, Hopkins, and candy bars also throw slick and far.

After the near phase-out of block tin, the most popular squid metals were chrome plate, stainless steel, or well-polished lead. There are occasions when a splash of color on the flanks or an overall paint job enhances appeal. Squids painted white, yellow, or blue have scored notable successes, and the hues of feather, hair, or synthetic dressing on a single upriding tail hook can make a crucial difference. Generally white, yellow, red and white, red and yellow, or green and white dressing is favored. Note that yellow is especially productive in murky water.

The hair from a whitetail deer's tail, as well as saddle hackle, once reigned supreme as dressing, but increasingly they have been replaced with synthetic fiber. Goat hair is not to be despised, for it is silky-smooth and long enough to complement any jig. Bucktail "breathes" in the water and seems to have an almost activated snowy glow, but it is destructible and prone to stain. Organic feathers have to be rinsed in fresh water after a sentimental journey, or they too begin to look cruddy and moth-eaten.

Sweeteners of limber pork rind, tailored either to a point or split, add a measure of come-hither wiggle and increase the apparent length of a given squid. Rind is available with a stinger hook to thwart the occasional short-striker, an addition we dislike because such a trailing barb has a tendency to lay back and foul in the process of casting.

Alterations and innovations are plentiful, yet few have become standard on the grounds. One, worthy of mention, is the Belmar Squid with a ring soldered far aft. To this ring is attached a short length of eelskin which wriggles enticingly. Curiously, this is one of the few tinclad types, although it is perhaps better called a combination, that has racked up notable catches of stripers at night. It is another of the one-time must-have lures now rarely employed.

We, together with Jack Townsend of Shrewbury, Massachusetts, once spent joyous workshop hours fashioning a squid graced by sparse tufts of bucktail strategically spaced amidships and glued into position. The idea was to simulate fins and the vague silhouette of backbone and rib cage showing through the almost transparent sides of small bait fishes. Our secret weapon cast like a sack of dry leaves and the bass perceptively ignored it.

A well-designed tinclad casts beautifully and is better suited than a plug to take stripers in violently clashing water. It also possesses pinpoint accuracy; the compact jig offers little air resistance when thrown hard, thus ensuring both range and flawless presentation. For want of a better phrase, positioning is rewarding, not only in hitting three inches from the corner of a clutching, weed-draped boulder, but in making use of every advancing ground swell. An accomplished squidder will engage his reel's clutch precisely at touchdown, *but not before* because that little error leads to stripped gears. With a little practice, the quick switch from free flight to solid control becomes almost automatic.

With a jig, and often with a plug, where steadily advancing ground swells are spilling over and tumbling forward, it is wise to drop the offering right behind the white horses and keep it swimming close to the tumble-down in the reverse slope of the wave. Wind-whipped spume, creaming suds, and ordinary turbulence do not create major problems, but a squid that is out of control on a slack line in rough water loses much of its attraction. Award top marks to that old angling injunction, "Keep a tight line."

Doodlebugs, barracudas, bullheads, bugeyes or lead-head jigs are one and the same. Nicknames are confusing: Bucktail is another of the favorites, a reminder of a time when most of these lures were dressed with hair from a deer's tail. Barracuda is one manufacturer's trade name. A doodlebug may be, especially to New Jersey anglers, either a lead-head, a surface-popping bug, or a cylindrical cork float used to keep bottom baits above cruising scavengers. On the Pacific Coast, the name "bullhead" conflicts with the common name of a little sculpin used as natural bait.

Whether we settle for bucktail or lead-head, one thing is certain: This lure is a proven killer of striped bass. Indeed there are well-educated marine anglers who avow that if they had to choose one artificial for all-round use in the salt, that lure would have to be a bucktail jig.

Basically, lead-head may be most the descriptive term since the classic configuration is a head made of that metal, bearing a fixed, single, upriding hook which is dressed with hair, feathers, and synthetic strands of the relatively new, soft plastic worm. Variations ranging from miniatures on up to foot-long models rigged with stinger hooks flood modern markets. Weight range is equally flexible, as are head shapes and color schemes. Among popular configurations are the fine lima-bean type, introduced by the late Morrie and Bill Upperman of New Jersey; bullet-nosed heads designed for deep jigging, trolling, or a hop-skip-jump progression over the bottom; horizontally flattened models to facilitate skimming over a shallow flat; and heads with diagonally cut faces that provide a small measure of built-in action. Chrome-plated, painted in every shade, sometimes fitted with sparkling glass eyes, each and every one of these basic types catch bass.

After so glowing a tribute, one may expect a caveat, so here it is. While all of the lead-heads are astonishingly versatile, each requires considerable angler skill to manipulate. Although the lima bean kicks like a frightened shrimp when given proper rod action, and the horizontally flattened types can be fluttered along a few inches over shoal bottoms, built-in action is sadly limited. You are going to "work" this lure, or you are going to go hungry. In many areas the greatest compliment you can pay to a marine angler is to say, "That character really knows how to use a bucktail jig!"

Lead-heads are effective 24 hours a day, in salt, brackish, or fresh water. They can be cast from shore or boat, trolled at any level, jigged deep, or switched along with the fast, erratic retrieve known as the Florida whip. Use them on soft line or wire as tackle and conditions dictate; on spinning, conventional, or offshore gear. In casting, for reasons which embrace range and rod work, the standard single-hooked jig is favored. This type also performs well when trolled offshore, although it is then in competition with the lengthier "nylon eels," the prototype of which is Tony Acetta's Jigit-Eel and is usually dressed with long filaments of nylon, armed with a stinger hook and, often, with a small Colorado spinner up front. Still a lead-head, this type is especially attractive to big stripers feeding just over the bottom or at mid-levels. Often an abbreviated, six- to eight-inch model is fitted with a single fixed hook.

In trolling, which is discussed at some length in the chapters dealing with boat fishing, regulars jig their lures continuously, thus imparting a seductive, hopping action. It is not profitable to be lazy and to merely drag these tempters over a feeding ground, but the jigging technqiue is an art to be learned, for it can be tremendously fatiguing. No written word is adequate to instruct; go out with an accomplished master and he will soon teach you how to coordinate arm, shoulder, back, and leg muscles in a steady, non-tiring, cadenced tempo.

Lures used in deep trolling include, top to bottom, nylon leadhead eel, swimming plug, and spoons of various sizes. These are used with barrel sinkers, on metal lines, or streamed from downriggers.

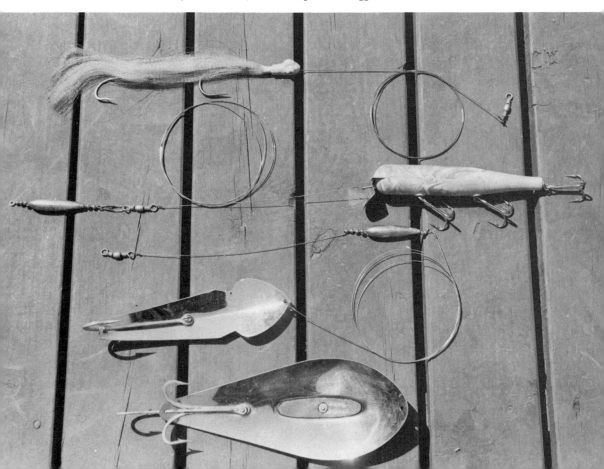

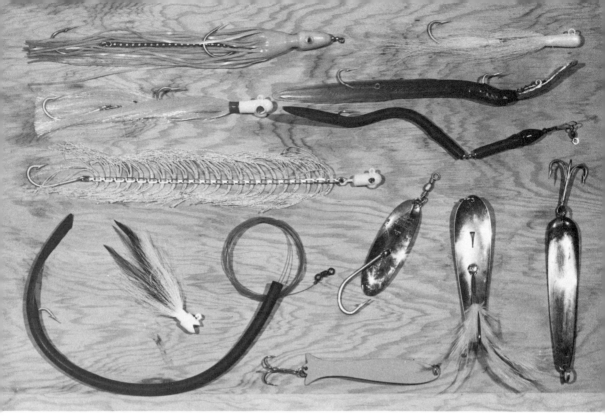

Trolling lures that are used include leadheads variously dressed, soft plastic eel or worm simulations, tube lures, and a variety of spoons.

The shore caster enjoys a variety of tactical possibilities. Indeed this artificial works at all levels besides the surface—and you can come pretty close to making it work there with a swift whip-retrieve. If you have selected the proper weight to complement a given tackle, a lead-head throws well and can be precisely right when bass are rushing small bait on the surface. Keep in mind another old adage to the effect that for every striper seen breaking water, there are nine under the ripples. Get a lure out there and bring it back fast with strenuous rod action to make the artificial dart, stop, dive, and zoom upward again.

A slow, hopping retrieve on bottom is effective when bass are feeding deep, and one can score while casting across a brisk current which runs roughly parallel to shore or guzzles out of an inlet. In this situation, the drill usually calls for a heave up and across the flow, followed by a steady jig retrieve as the lead-head swings down to that point where it leaves pay-off territory and swings into shallow water. As with any artificial, bring-back is best slowed at night.

It is likely that all-white or all-yellow jigs take a majority of striped bass, but every color in the spectrum has a place. Glass or painted eyes may catch more fishermen than fish, and there's some argument about the need for delicate paint jobs or scale finishes on heads. In hard bottom-bouncing, enamel soon wears off, but the bass never complain, for they zero in on the

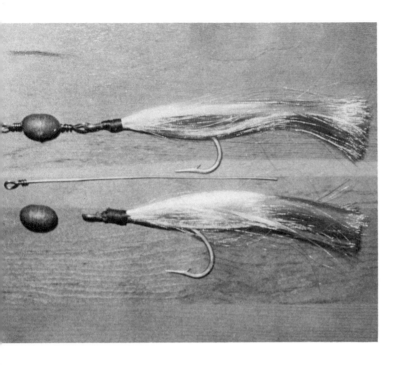

A deep-going nylon eel lure is easily constructed in your home workshop. The ingredients are a hook of proper size, dressing material, winding thread, a length of wire leader material, and a pierced egg sinker.

trailing dressing. Soft plastic worms, curly-tails, or whatever the local moniker or trade name, are increasingly popular in lieu of dressing. They are lively in the water, inexpensive, available in a multitude of colors and lengths, and can be replaced in seconds if they tear under a hard strike or are shredded by sharp-toothed interlopers. Lead-heads are not all-purpose; nothing is. But in the hands of an educated angler, this hunk of lead and wisp of dressing may come closest to that description.

Tradition dies hard and no master of the tin squid or bucktail ever admits that his classic technique has been challenged. However, today's striped bass enthusiasts heartily endorse plugs, some of them to the exclusion of all other artificials. Although an advanced angler uses every tempter in a considerable arsenal, it is true that plugs are wonderfully versatile: They are quite as effective by day or by night, when cast from shore or boat, trolled on the surface or in the depths.

The modern plug is, of course, an American invention. Jim Heddon may have known about the early Indian use of carrot-shaped lengths of pine or spruce stained with vegetable dyes, but Heddon is credited with introducing the current prototype as a killer of fresh water black bass. Our present version moved into salt water by a roundabout route, through the brackish streams of the Deep South, where it proved valuable on snook, small tarpon, weakfish, and a host of other sheltered fresh water gamesters.

Along the North Atlantic seaboard, striped bass fishermen initiated their plug casting with lures originally designed for muskelunge. During World War II the musky-sized Creek Chub Pikie Minnow was so popular a lure on Massachusetts' Cape Cod Canal that stocks were swiftly depleted and single baits were worth whatever owners might demand.

The Pikie was considered unbeatable at the time, and it was used as a surface splasher. Its wobble-plate was bent straight so that the lure would not dive and swim as intended, but would thrash and struggle on top. Although light for the heavy conventional surf rods then in use, Pikie took many hundreds of fish and went into partial eclipse only when larger and more "castable" creations appeared on the scene.

Even prior to that turn-about around 1946, at least one large plug was on the market—South Bend's Tarp-Oreno, a beefed-up copy of the firm's excellent little Bass-Oreno. It was about eight inches long and fitted with two huge Sobey hooks, each large enough to subdue a trophy tuna. There seems to be no evidence to indicate that the South Bend plug ever made waves among

A shoal of plugs—and one soft plastic eel with a wobble plate. All account for good striper catches.

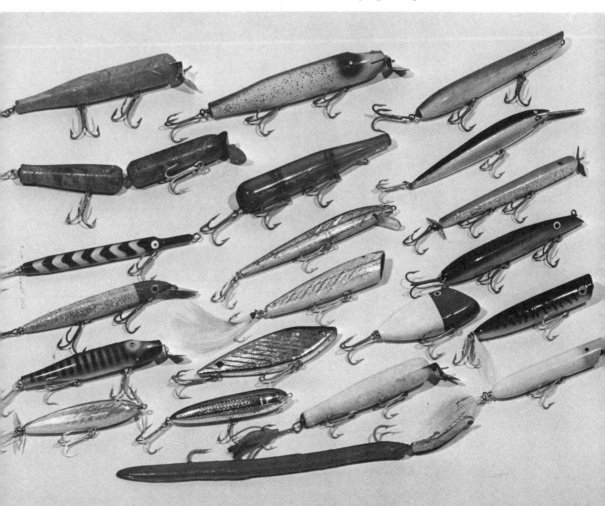

serious striper fishermen, but it would take bass. We field-stripped one, fitted it with 5/0 trebles instead of the big Sobeys, and it worked well.

Unfortunately there were not many "store-bought" plugs available in 1946, so most of the fishermen who had trained on inland black bass home-crafted mammoth facsimiles of fresh water favorites. Among the first was the "broomstick," so called because it was actually whittled from a broom handle and angle-cut at the head so that it would splash during surface retrieve. Cleaned up and improved upon, this early killer evolved as Stan Gibbs' justly famous Castalure, which is still much used.

Magically, with that first rush to salt water, a growing number of new lures reached a seller's market. The worst of them were better than anything yet designed for striper fishing, and the best are still treasured. In the beginning, partly because tackle was designed to throw considerable weight, bulk was necessary—and yet there was much suspicion of large plugs. Bob Pond's original Striper Atom was eight inches long, and many thought that too big to succeed. That it succeeded exceptionally well is now history, and the Atom is currently offered in various size ranges.

Other early favorites were the Cap'n Bill's Swimmer, Jerry's Flaptail, and larger editions of the timeless Pikie Minnow. Poppers earned swift acceptance, but today's fine darting plugs were not yet in existence. Nobody had then heard of Rapala's balsa-wood Finnish minnow, now widely copied and tremendously popular among light tackle buffs.

Every tackle shop now offers a multitude of different plugs, yet most of them are variations of old stand-bys. They are better than the originals, but nothing space-age or startling. In the hundreds currently available it is almost impossible to find a genuine new departure. There are, if logically divided into categories, about seven different configurations: surface swimmers, sub-surface swimmers, darters, surface commotion baits, sliders, torpedoes, and the Finnish minnow. Each type may be varied so that it offers an individual nuance of action, but a surface swimmer remains just that, whether it is jointed, foreshortened or elongated, artistically finished, weighted at some salient point, or trailing a dressing. The creation is a surface swimmer if it swims on the surface.

Sub-surface swimmers travel under water, usually at a pre-determined depth controlled by weighting, the angle of the wobble-plates, the speed of a trolling boat, or the tempo of a retrieve. Darters are close relatives, differing only in that they exhibit a definite darting motion and often require more inspired rod handling in order to excel. We hasten to mention that "Darter" is a copyrighted trade name of the Creek Chub Company. This firm made one of the first and best of the type in a small size, a lure still in service everywhere.

Surface commotion lures, as the term implies, make a lot of fuss on top. These include poppers and splashers, together with a few close cousins that

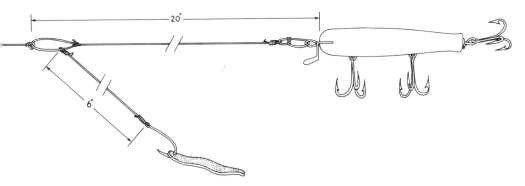

A pork-rind dropper positioned ahead of a plug is a rig that is effective on the surface or at any level. A fly or bait strip may be substituted for the pork rind.

These additions are designed to impart greater action to a plug. Top to bottom: a bucktail teaser fastened with a stainless steel staple; a pork-rind strip or strip of cut bait added to the tail hook; an eelskin drawn over the plug and secured at the head (Split-shank or open-eye treble hooks may be used for this combination); bucktail or nylon "fins" attached to the shoulders of the lure ("Fins" are of special value when stripers are chasing whiting).

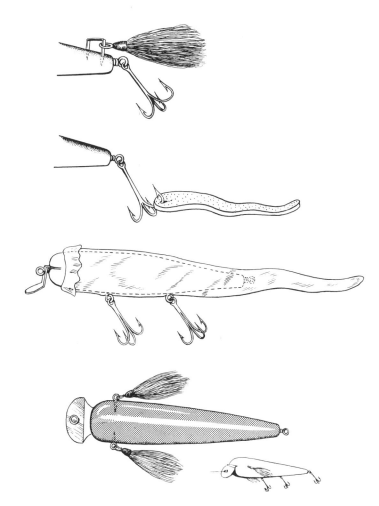

combine the actions of the true popper and the slider. Examples of this latter bait would include the squid-simulating Reverse Atom and the lean Gibbs Pencil Popper.

Sliders, often called "stick baits," are activated by rod work alone. They are made to dance on the surface or, in weighted models, to progress under water in a series of angler-directed starts and stops. They are slim and elongated to simulate a sand eel or one of the half-beaks. Boone's Needlefish is a good example, as are the Heddon Zara Spook and the Pflueger Ballerina— although the last named pair of dancers are not elongated; they are roughly cigar-shaped and, properly employed, draw savage strikes.

Torpedo plugs, for want of a better name, are those designed to work beneath the surface, aided by clever rod handling. Among them one must list the fine Mirrolure, which, although it has attained its greatest fame in tropical waters, effectively seduces bass in colder seas. Some of these torpedo types are fitted with spinners at nose and tail to add flash, but not swimming action. Spinners are also fitted on some of the surface sliders, in which case they add flash to commotion.

It can be argued that the Finnish minnow is nothing other than a sub-surface swimmer—and some models are designed to wriggle along on top— but Rapala and a host of near look-alikes are in a class by themselves. They execute a rapid, nervous wriggle when trolled or retrieved, not at all similar to the average snakey action of the basic swimmer. They are, in the most efficient of fish-catching series, exasperatingly light and difficult to cast a great distance.

One other type might be mentioned, a fairly recent maverick developed by surfmen on the Island of Nantucket and initially called the Rabbit. Now more generally known as the Ballistic, this lure is made by a few home craftsmen who are more interested in tempting bluefish than striped bass. Ballistic is a flattened, elongated lure, a tin squid with a wooden skin: it casts better than any true plug and planes on the surface when retrieved at high speed.

We conclude that there are seven basic types although it is readily apparent that this figure may be argued. Fortunately, all of the top-ranking bass plugs are made in a variety of sizes and weights. Wooden lures are still marketed, although the trend is toward hard plastic, solid or compartmented. At long last makers have been convinced that marine fishing requires stout rigging and hooks designed for work, not the inland tweaking of tiddlers. Color systems are multitudinous, with simulations of just about every forage bait, plus some unlikely and garish combinations that occasionally seem irresistible.

There are exceptions, but poppers and other surface commotion lures are most effective in daylight hours, while swimmers, darters, torpedoes, and Finnish minnows work under the sun or the stars. Every plug features its own most practical rate of retrieve or trolling speed, yet the rule of thumb is "slower at night." Regardless of the rule, if a suggested pace fails to draw strikes, try another.

There is a popular misconception to the effect that any lure boasting built-in action needs no "rod work," and it is a fact that you will tie into stripers while simply throwing it out and reeling it in. You will get far more by adding manipulation, perhaps a sudden pop followed by a pause, short bursts of speed, a painful wriggle forward; then repeat the sequence. Occasionally one may succeed with no retrieve at all! One night a half-dozen of us were flogging the surf on a strong moon tide with a heavy current sweeping down parallel to the beach. Nobody had reported so much as a half-hearted strike until one of the party landed three glistening middleweights in succession. The man was laconic. He said, "Walk the plug."

It turned out that he was throwing diagonally up and across the flow, at touchdown retrieving just enough slack to maintain contact. Then he trudged down the shingle, striving to match the current speed. His swimming plug was not progressing shoreward, but was swinging in an arc, wriggling in that turbulent flood, and simulating an injured bait fish borne along on the surface. We copycats swiftly learned to walk a plug.

On site and prior to action, nurture a passionate love for sharp hooks. A fine-edged bastard file touches up points in seconds, a chore that pays off in sure hooking. A lot of regulars not only sharpen constantly, but mash each barb flat. This ensures slicker and deeper penetration, presents no handicap when a line is kept taut, and facilitates release where that is desired.

On-site alterations can be a blessing or just the opposite, since every addition or subtraction will materially change a plug's action. Strip lead wound around the hook shanks at a swimmer's center of gravity will certainly slow the artificial, but not as drastically as it would if it were placed aft. A popper *should* have added weight at the tail, if such weight seems necessary in order to attain distance. Wobble-plates may be slightly bent, up or down, thus changing a lure's performance. Bend the plug's pull-wire eye down and the artificial will swim higher in the water; up, and it pursues a deeper path. Tail hooks can be dressed, fitted with free-swinging tufts of hair or feathers or maybe a single pork rind. This adds a bit of seductive motion aft, yet still slows the overall action.

Skin-plugs, aptly named and often deadly on night or day tides, are prepared by encasing a swimmer with the flexible skin of an eel. Remove all hooks, draw the skin over the plug's body and tie it at the head. Replace first and second trebles with open-eye types and either add a single hook aft or use none. You want three to four inches of tapered eel tail left to wriggle enticingly. It is quite possible that the texture of a fresh, wet skin prevents the bass from spitting out the plug, just as certain soft plastic lures apparently dupe a fish because it thinks it has latched on to a bona fide sea creature. A few rabid enthusiasts are sure that the skin, in addition to its other virtues, also exudes an attractive scent.

Combinations of plugs and dropper files are particularly effective at night, though less attractive by day. Position a basic fly on a dropper loop at the forward end of the leader, or simply tie in a single 6/0 hook on which is impaled a strip of pork rind. Do not worry about the dropper loop's tendency to wrap around the leader. Bass do not seem to mind and they often prefer the small tempter to the larger one swimming aft. It was precisely this combination, with a live eel instead of a plug, which accounted for Tony Stetzko's 73-pound surf striper in the fall of 1981.

Another combination rig, first popularized on northern striper grounds by the late, great Jerry Sylvester of Narragansett, Rhode Island, and actually a spin-off of the old Southern popping-cork-and-shrimp approach, is an unarmed splasher trailed by a length of leader tipped with a fly, a pork rind strip or a small lead-head jig. This can be highly effective on school stripers in shoal water during daylight hours. Its major handicap is a tendency to foul during the cast.

While a number of artificials, including lead-head types and plugs are equally efficient whether cast or trolled, some—like the tin squid which is always best when cast—are to a considerable degree specialized. Spoons are not often encountered on a sea beach, yet trolled they rank among the finest of striper producers. There are a number of types and variations, ranging from tiny wobblers on up to the huge bunker spoon, which imitates a struggling menhaden or herring. Count among the proven models Acetta Pet, Huntington Drone, Pflueger Record, and Chum. These may be painted or anodized to provide flashes of color, yet they are more often chrome-plated. A few are subtly scale-finished.

Hooks, usually fixed and riding upright, are also free-swinging in some proven models. A majority are singles. The pie plate-sized bunker spoon often sports a brace of big singles rigged like ice tongs on a welded split ring. There is considerable use of pork rind, either the small prepared strips or the larger and more imaginative teasers cut to shape by canny skippers and mates.

Offshore trollers tempt a few stripers with that almost universal favorite, the Japanese Feather; yet this has never proved as effective a lure on bass as spoons, surgical tube lures, versions of the lead-head nylon eel, soft plastic rubber worms, eel and squid imitations, and the bulky, so-called "umbrella." This last is a modern adaptation of the old Chesapeake Bay spreader, normally armed with four small surgical tubes on radiating outrigger wires, together with a centrally streamed lure, which may be another tube or a swimming plug. Invariably deep-trolled, the umbrella is a bass killer; yet it requires the use of heavy tackle and must be handled with care when an active fish is brought aboard and those flying hooks threaten human flesh.

Surgical tubes are relatively new arrivals and have become welcome standards, used at all levels. Action is a sinuous weaving, looping motion

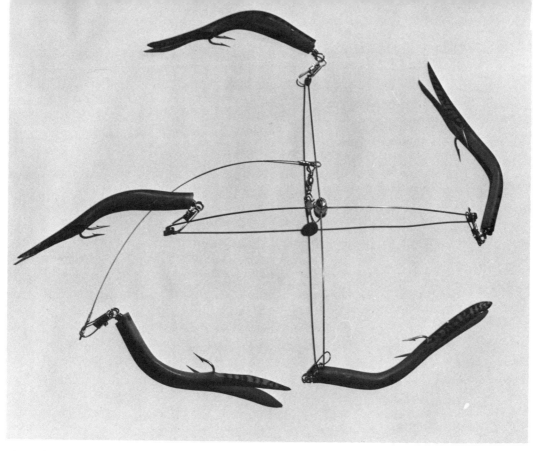

A spreader, also called an "umbrella rig," is often armed with split-tailed tube lures, but may have a plug or other lure as a central attractor.

which often seems irresistible to bass. A few shorties, fitted with lead-heads, serve beach casters when sand eels are in the wash. A fair share of the longer offshore tubes are also weighted forward.

Among big bass killers there exists a fine company of soft plastic trolling lures fabricated to simulate squid, eels, or seaworms. There are two basic types—one fitted with a lead-head and used much as is the nylon eel, in a close-to-bottom or mid-level jigging operation; the other boasting a molded-in or stamped wobble plate. All are effective 24 hours a day.

Curiously, aside from limited use in sheltered waters, spinners have yet to attain any massive popularity in the salt. At one time a double-bladed willow-leaf type was much used ahead of a trolled sea worm, but one sees little of this efficient combination today. It is safe to predict that there will be future imaginative and successful utilization of spinners. Another possible striper tempter, not yet exploited to any extent on this species, is the Pacific Coast herring dodger, which is used as a flashing attractor ahead of bait or lure to catch salmon. Logically, like the huge eastern bunker spoon, the concept might score well on grounds where big bass are seasonal visitors.

Artificial lures may not yet rival natural baits in point of numbers used, yet they have become the beloved tools of a legion of new classicists on American striper coasts.

Stripers dote on the turbulent water around rock pile, so jetty jockeys find such spots alluring also. Photo by Vlad Evanoff.

7 · The High Surf

IF THERE IS AN ARISTOCRACY OF ZEALOTS AMONG striped bass fishermen, it is surely made up of those hardy, adventurous souls who tackle the high surf. Wading into action day and night, breasting ice-cold combers, clambering over the most subversively slippery rocks in the world and enduring fatigue that would kill an ordinary citizen, the confirmed surfman is forever optimistic. He is a pure fanatic, endlessing searching for the wild excitement of a thing called "blitz."

In surf casting jargon, a "blitz" is defined as a period of magnificent striper fishing—a half-hour, an hour, or even a whole tide in which bass compete with one another for the dubious honor of smashing at natural or artificial baits tossed into the hissing brine. This happens when the complex chemistry of marine life and the elements is happily mixed, subtly blended and served up in one grand riot of teeming bait, screaming birds, and frantically feeding fish.

Let us, however, reach a basic understanding. No one, present company included, has ever been able to state flatly that stripers will oblige at any specific time or place. Nonetheless, veterans usually turn up wherever and whenever the fish are hitting. That is because they observe certain general rules which are compounded of many things: the characteristics of the fish itself, weather conditions, tides, the movement of bait—and the success or failure of yesterday's anglers.

Our purpose here is to discuss these general rules and to enlarge upon the secrets of the successful high-surf fisherman. His magic touch is based upon knowledge, plus skill in the employment of various lures and baits. Luck plays an infinitesimal part in the consistent success of a surf caster. There are no "lucky fishermen," although there are many who have been lucky on occasion.

The formula is simplicity itself: Find a fish and offer it a natural bait or artificial which awakens its hunger or stirs the critter to green-eyed rage. Unfortunately, the first requirement may be the most difficult to fulfill. The most obvious of the short cuts to finding bass is careful scrutiny of the rod and gun columns in your local newspapers; still better, a short conversation with a brother angler who was "there yesterday." Charter skippers and coastal bait dealers are usually well-informed and anxious to keep anglers posted.

In the hard-fished sections, the Montauks, Cape Cods, and San Franciscos, an army of angling fanatics are in constant touch with the situation. Although individuals who discover fast action are apt to maintain strict secrecy, information invariably leaks. Beach buggy skippers not only watch each other; some of them fly daily reconnaissance missions out of local airports. Thus, all of the regulars know, almost to the tide, where pods of bass are feeding and loafing. Bait shops and sporting goods dealers relay that information to visitors.

There is, of course, the occasional liveryman, outdoor writer, or tackle tycoon who is out of immediate contact with the picture, but is anxious to justify his reputation, or rent his boats, by supplying some sort of information. Since the worth of any striper report must be measured by its timeliness, beware of the lad who is vague about *when* they hit, *where* they hit, and *what* they hit. Pay undivided attention to the on-site agent who can tell you that a certain section of beach yielded bass yesterday; that the fish were banging specific lures on specific tides; and that anglers, whose names he is able to quote, landed respectable catches.

This is the sort of intelligence you want, yet there is the problem of narrowing your search to perhaps a half-mile of beach, a rip, an offshore bar, or a deep blue hole where the great linesides munch on a variety of seafood. Will they hit on night or day tides? When, and where, and on which lures? For the beginner, that vast and winking ocean often appears to be a biological desert. He arrives, like as not, at high noon and dead-low tide. Bone-weary gladiators rest on the high dunes after a long night in the roaring suds. The gulls and terns are silent; even the air is sultry and oppressive. A vast, blue-green sea stretches away to benign infinity. Can this be the spot where huge stripers are waiting for well presented baits?

It can be, and often is, but the action may await a more favorable tide, a movement of bait, or a mystic hour when all sea creatures are charged with vitality. If you know the surf and its changing moods, you will be able to read the signs and make decisions; if you are an admitted beginner, there is a happy alternative. Simply strike up an oblique conversation with one of the local loungers. Don't ask him where to fish. Let him tell *you* how the bass rushed bait at yesterday evening's high tide, how he hooked a monster and was cleaned out—surface plug, line, and the hope of a new record!

Prior to low-key interrogation of salty acquaintances, it is wise to join a home-town striper fishing club. These organizations are proliferating, peopled by armies of neophytes and a far smaller gaggle of blooded experts who will volunteer shop-talk and, possibly, invite you to accompany them on forthcoming sentimental journeys. In no time at all the lingo will become understandable and you will know what a grizzled character means when he

Not dangerous, just uncomfortable. Surf casters often must cope with big, bursting combers.

grunts, "Good moon tide Saturday. Flood at dawn, so if there's no fire in the water. . ."

Tides run high course during a full moon period. Flood means high water and may be referred to as a "good tide" when currents are surging in the pre-dawn darkness. Fire is the eerie glow emitted by disturbed diatoms, a curiously bright phenomenon that handicaps nighttime surf fishing. Few regulars are fond of "fire."

This, admittedly, is kindergarten instruction, although it does comprise the ABC's of surf casting for striped bass. Having acquired suitable tackle and learned how to use it, education proceeds at flank speed. First off, although it is possible and occasionally most practical to use other outfits in the high surf, successful beachcombers place most of their trust in lengthy, relatively heavy rods mounting conventional or spinning reels. It is not that these sticks are the best of fish-fighting instruments: They are designed to throw, because if you cannot drop lure or bait on a fairly distant target, then strikes may be few and far between. A rod length of, say, 10½ to 11 feet for revolving-spool and up to 14 feet for spinning gear, aids heaving and also keeps running line over the top of advancing wave crests.

Line tests will depend on individual preference, the forgiving resilience of a given rod, and angler skill. Basically, surf spinning enthusiasts consider 15-pound-test monofilament a sort of starting point, although some heavier strands and some much lighter ones are employed. Years ago, 36-pound-test linen twist, and then a nylon braid of comparable clout, were deemed classics in conventional squidding. Now the norm appears to be 30-pound mono. With any light strand, the fisherman should employ a shock leader of heavier weight and long enough to provide adequate casting hang-over from the tip top, to go back through the guides, and to make a few turns around the reel's spool. The shocker is designed to serve as a basic leader in itself but, more importantly, to survive stress when a big rod is loaded in throwing. Wire leaders are passé, since monofilament is tough enough to absorb minor punishment from a striper's sandpaper-lined jaws and is easier to knot into running line. Use a minimum of hardware: at the maximum a neat and well-locking terminal snap to attach a lure, or a barrel swivel, fishfinder rig and specialized sinker to ensure best results in bottom-baiting.

So far as we know, the term "high surf" is our invention. In the jargon of sport fishing, at least, the definition we suggested to IGFA and promptly adopted in an association glossary is "Heavy surf on an open ocean beach." This is intended to differentiate between mill-pond conditions and furious lines of breakers where the sea gets a running start before it throws a holiday punch ashore.

Initially, and you can do this on any spacious field where no ribald kibitzers will guffaw as a fledgling suffers backlash or line slough, learn to cast without undue difficulty. Never attempt to match the experts from scratch;

throw short at first and gradually lengthen your succeeding efforts. Libraries are loaded with books detailing the standard techniques, and these will help. For openers, stick with the easy, close-to-overhand power drive which is smoothly accelerated from inception through rod loading to release, mentally accepting the fact that there will be ample time in the future to experiment with more sophisticated casting techniques. Use an unarmed plug or a dipsey sinker as terminal weight. Where at all possible, enlist the aid of a local surfman who will guide gently. Really, it is quite simple, nothing more than an extension of inland plug casting or spinning.

Once the rig becomes tractable, and that does not take long, strive for distance, not because bass always cartwheel way out there, but because the capability to throw far will ensure a flawless performance at the usually shorter effective ranges. Strive for nail-driving accuracy, a skill that pays off when a lure must be dropped right onto a promising swirl, at the edge of a mussel bed, or within inches of a weedy, barnacle-encrusted boulder.

There is ample choice of lures, and we discuss these in another chapter. However, do not be conned into ordering a high-priced "secret killer" of the type usually advertised in non-sporting publications as "guaranteed to catch fish." A rigged cigar will also catch fish, but not very often—and a cheap cigar costs far less than any flim-flam artist's sucker bait.

Every well-educated surf caster takes certain short cuts to good fishing when he visits a strange beach. The difference between the expert and the amateur is that the former immediately builds a personal dossier of information that will serve as a future guide. In addition to all the striper lore which he has stockpiled over the years, this man will recognize the necessity to evaluate bottom conformation and feeding grounds; the need to understand local weather conditions and how prevailing winds make or break the sport; which baits or lures are likely to be successful, and why.

It is quite impossible to declare any wind direction or velocity as ideal on all sea beaches, for what is most propitious varies from strand to strand. Where productive bars lie well offshore, a wind at one's back helps to loft a long cast, but often a gale right in the teeth will move both bait and bass so close that a wader may feel them bumping against his legs. There are also provincial breezes to contend with. On the big beaches ranging south of San Francisco, for example, a near-gale in the face is close to normal. Outer Cape Cod, during the summer months, is more likely to boast sou'west zephyrs that permit a relative duffer to perform like a tournament caster. "It all depends on how the wind blows" may be true enough, but that which is most attractive on one sea rim may be bad news on another.

Anglers who seek striped bass generally feel that sport will peak two hours before the top of the tide and two hours afterward, with perhaps an hour's or more hiatus at slack flood or ebb while the ocean is shifting gears. Tides build the currents and bass like moving water, hence one expects the best results during periods of strong ebb and flow, which are accurately charted in government tide and current tables. Abnormal wind conditions or storms will change tidal schedules by as much as an hour, but this is natural trickery.

While a building flood enjoys angler acclaim, ebb can be quite as productive, particularly when small bait are pouring out of a canal, river, or inlet as the pulsing sea retreats. In such areas stripers invariably line up to feast on a veritable smörgasbord borne along on the surging out-flow. One also learns to visit rips that are reachable from shore at those stages of the tide when bottom conformation, currents, and winds combine to create bait-tumbling turbulence. Being in the right spot at the right time becomes far easier after one has studied a given location and jotted down, either in memory or in a well-kept daily log, conditions likely to obtain as history repeats.

Each coastal section observes seasons within seasons, since stripers are largely migratory and are affected by water temperature and availability of bait. There is almost a calendar date of arrival and departure at every seaboard, a buildup toward peak, and a climax of spray-laced action after which the tapering-off is rapid. Usually, daytime sport is best in spring and fall. When high summer pressure-cooks a famous bassing ground, stripers become progressively nocturnal. (See the chapter entitled *Striper Fisherman's Calendar* for times and places.)

Hot spots on any coast will feature sand beaches, leagues of jumbled rock piles, or a combination of the two. There are sharp drop-offs and long, shallow slopes descending to blue water, furious surf, and sections where seasonal "regulation winds" keep smashing combers to more or less mild dimensions. Add current clashes where tidal flows converge; river mouths, inlets, offshore bars, man-made canals, and jetties constructed by *Homo sapiens*, but tastefully adorned by Poseidon with barnacles and weed that pastures a host of small sea creatures that attract hungry bass.

Obviously, the best time to examine a beach is at dead-low tide, and the ideal observation post is an elevation such as a high dune or bank. Then, while the sea is drawing a deep breath, study the bottom conformation with the aid of polarized glasses and binoculars. File for future reference the precise location of grass and shell beds, mud flats where clams, crabs, shrimp, and sea worms are likely to abide, and points of land where interesting little tide rips will build as currents accelerate. Every rockpile is a potential bonanza, whether located so that it is below or rises above the surface. That is where stripers will hold to feast on befuddled forage.

Roccus—we continue to use the discarded Latin—is robust, powerful, and rarely seems discomfitted by sand suspended in raging water. Schoolies, being young, athletic, and lighthearted, are likely to drive bait right into the wash. Larger fish prefer to stooge around offshore bars or drop-offs during the daylight hours, yet they also prowl close to the shingle at night or in stormy weather. When heavyweights crowd the shore, they almost always arrive by way of cuts which have been punched through outer bars.

White water, no matter how furious it seems, is potent ground for schoolies and middleweights—the mecca of the clever squidder throwing metal jigs. Big fish are taken in this witch's cauldron as well, yet they are more likely to cruise the edges or lumber around relatively deep grass and mussel beds where the living is easy. These old bass are lazy and selective. That is how they got to be record-breakers in the first place.

Their selectivity cannot be over-emphasized. Stripers of any size are likely to feed collectively on a single bait species for a specific period of time, after which they become jaded and concentrate on another. Often there is no use at all in offering a mackerel if the cusses are conditioned to squid. Then it is the better part of valor to accept the inevitable and to tempt them with natural squid or a facsimile thereof. This mercurial switching of appetite is always a factor. On many North Atlantic beaches, when raging storms litter the high tide line with sea clams torn from the bottom, bass—sometimes for several consecutive days—acquire an overwhelming taste for rancid clam flesh that is returned to the inshore grounds by the successive rise and fall of the tide. When that happens, the odds are three to one that a surf caster had best forget other baits and artificial lures. Nobody has yet invented a plug that looks like a clam, especially a clam *sans* shell making its current-induced way back into the graveyard of the deep, so a wise surfman will gather whatever natural bits of the preferred bait he can.

"Good water," a term loosely employed, may mean that the sea is clear, choppy, roiled by tide rips, or simply pleasing to the eye of an angler. Clarity is relative, although stripers prefer a measure of cleanliness. Live water is always preferable to that which is still. Weeds, floating free after stormy weather, or the marine algae blooms that irk anglers and foul hooks do not adversely affect bass. On the contrary, these fish sometimes feed most avidly in cluttered areas. When weed is thick close inshore, it is often possible to cast beyond the goglum and enjoy dirt-free retrieve up to the barrier. Any fish hooked outside the garbage is sure to pick up an apparent ton of the stuff as it is pumped shoreward. It is an occupational hazard. With weed or nighttime "fire," figure that the area will be cleared as though by magic at the turn of the tide. This is not a sure thing, but it often happens.

Elemental fury is unwelcome, but does not always dictate abject failure. It is well-documented that bass often feed heavily just before and just after a murderous coastal storm. Almost certainly these genetically imprinted fishes respond to changing barometric pressures and, sensing a smashing gale before it arrives, stuff themselves with bait and loaf until the elements relent. It is logical to expect renewed action after the winds shift and the ocean quits threatening to engulf all *terra firma*. We have caught stripers at midnight during a spectacular electrical storm, but we do not recommend fishing under such conditions. We also once hooked and landed a bass during that poisonously unreal hour or so of deceptive calm in the "eye" of a hurricane. As an aside, there is no truth in the ancient nonsense that stripers gulp stones to provide ballast in a rough sea. Stones and weed growth *are* found in their stomachs, having been accidentally ingested while grubbing the bottom for more digestible foodstuffs.

Smart surf fishermen are well-informed, but they take nothing completely for granted. The fish is so delightfully unpredictable that an angler must be something of an opportunist: He cannot afford to decide that a particular tide is always wrong. A sudden influx of bait can, and frequently does, blow all generalizations into the well-known cocked hat. Some of the best fishing we have ever lucked into occurred during periods when no one expected to see, much less catch, a bass. This is a rare treat and one of the phenomenons that keeps a surfman forever on his toes, watching for the first hint of incipient action.

The signs are unmistakable once you know what to look for. It may be nothing more than a tern that pauses in its swallowlike flight to circle and hover. It can be a sudden flipping of small bait or the telltale bulge of a lineside feeding just below the surface. The appearance of a rapidly spreading slick in otherwise choppy water often means that a pod of bass is located just below the ripples. Finally, every salt-crusted regular on the coast can *smell* stripers. The scent is variously described and thyme is often mentioned. It is not "dead fish," and a surfman may only whiff the fragrance when a breeze is quartering inshore. Anyone can distinguish the fresh, pleasant scent that a striper exudes when first brought to beach, but only veterans locate them with a trained nose.

During years of fishing an angler may see an occasional lineside come clear in a clean, salmonlike leap. It is a rarity, for they are not accomplished jumpers. More often evidence is posted by a sudden concentration of birds, terns or laughing gulls circling like so many fighter planes, dipping and even diving beneath the surface. They seldom plunge when bluefish are present. Larger gulls, clumsy by comparison with their smaller cousins, are equal indicators of turmoil below.

Beachcombing types pay rapt attention to shoals of bait, with or without birds overhead. Squid shoot out of the water like so many tawny torpedoes. Mackerel take evasive action in a nervous, rustling surface commotion. Spearing twinkle like a charge of silvery buckshot. Menhaden flurry wildly, flashing brassy flanks and creating a miniature surf of their own. Mullet dart and leap in broken showers of quicksilver.

At night, when hungry linesides prowl close to shore, their presence is indicated by sand eels, tiny bait fish of all types, and squid gasping on a hostile shingle. There is usually enough available light to see these stranded creatures, or even to hear them above the metronomic boom, slide, and pause

Herring gulls hover over baitfish being driven to the surface by hungry bass.

Circling, diving birds are sure signs of feeding bass. Surf casters hasten to those areas where there is "bird action."

of surf. If you opt to use a light, shield the beam and use it sparingly; otherwise neighboring anglers are sure to mutter hard words. Few, other than stationary bottom fishermen on a beach, feel that lights aid their cause.

Of course, any of the marine forage species may be chased by fish other than striped bass but, if the action is at all hot, you will not be kept in doubt. Stripers hit the surface in an angry, boiling eruption, swapping ends, slapping broad tails, and creating lingering bursts of white foam. Get there fast, make a short heave to wet the line, and then lay a pinpoint shot right into that wild commotion. Two to one you will register a jarring strike that will make all of the waiting, the study, and the weariness worth while.

Surf casting can be a 24-hour proposition, but nevertheless a sizeable contingent of addicts prefer to scour beaches from dawn to sunset, rising and retiring with the birds. Other incurables, particularly on the Atlantic seaboard, swear by the hours of darkness. There is much to be said for either choice, plus an accolade to those hot-eyed fanatics who work the optimum tides both night and day, almost literally sleeping, at fitful intervals, with eyes open and fixed on the surf. Although fatiguing, it pays to be versatile.

Elsewhere in this book we discuss artificial lures and natural baits, plus techniques for using them, and there is no profit in repetition. However, no matter what the offering, a surf caster must conquer one final hurdle before he can apply for record or even boast modestly about his prowess in the suds or sit down to a gourmet seafood dinner. He has to land a hooked warrior.

Whether you tie into a surf-running striper on a tin squid, a plug, or a tempting morsel of natural bait, the game is the same—a vigorous battle which must be fought intelligently to avoid abrasive contact with rock piles, to tire the prize, and to lead it through a steadily marching line of breakers to a safe haven ashore. It begins with the strike itself, solid and reassuring, but that is only the beginning. Almost always a bass is most securely hooked on a metal squid or other lure armed with a single barb. The treble hooks that adorn a majority of plugs are never as efficient, for each works against another and a cartwheeling, furiously thrashing gamester is apt to dislodge them.

Every fishing season witnesses a sorry percentage of poor souls who are "cleaned out" by huge stripers that hit, run, and keep right on running after a line parts. Such a thing is excusable only if a bass is stuck at the very end of a long cast and if the angler's line is shorter than it should be. A particularly active striper of more than 30 pounds conceivably may dash 50 yards in one sustained drive, but few uncork sizzling straight-away runs. The cleaning out is most likely on that aforementioned heroic throw to a bright horizon, after which a hooked wrestler is aided by a strong current racing offshore from the edge of a rip.

One well-remembered night we came very close to losing all of our string under such conditions. With visions of a trophy flickering through our sweaty consciousnesses, we thought it a blessing when the heavyweight slowed, held for an agonizing few minutes, and then began to yield. Usually, it is worth noting, a seasoned surfman is able to guess the approximate bulk of a striper by the sort of fight it wages. This one proved a disappointment, for it scaled an ounce under 50 pounds and was just another "good fish."

While the current all-tackle world's record of 76 pounds was boated at Montauk, New York, such heavyweights are far from off-limits to a surf angler. On the night of November 3, 1981, Tony Stetzko of Orleans, Massachusetts, beached a 73-pounder at Nauset Beach, a Cape Cod hot spot located in the townships of Orleans and Chatham. No exact location was reported, but the fish was hooked from shore on a combination consisting of a live eel with a 6-inch, black dropper "fly" positioned ahead of it. The bass took the dropper, not the eel, and was landed on 17-pound-test monofilament.

Stetzko's prize, at this writing the largest striper ever brought to account by a surf caster, was an opportunity strike, since Tony had planned only to catch a few of the codfish then characteristically feeding close to the dunes. Knowing that a few king-sized bass had been taken during the preceeding week, he went to the eel-and-dropper rig and scored almost immediately. The monster made three powerful runs but was landed within 15 minutes.

Stripers are really at their fighting best between 25 to 40 pounds. Over that weight bracket they tend toward sluggishness, with bulldog power, but are seldom fast or acrobatic. A very big fish runs a short distance, sounds, shakes its head, turns sideways in the current and, for a time, resists all angler effort. Smaller bass often cartwheel on the surface, particularly in shallow water. Large or small, the initial and most spectacular drive will not be straight out to sea, but more or less parallel to the shore. It is necessary to maintain a tight line and to apply healthy, but reasonable, drag pressure.

High on the list of reasons why bass pop lines is a tight drag. The star on a conventional reel or the adjustable drag in spinning should be snugged up only to that point where the resulting tension will set sharp hooks. There should be no further tightening of the brake during a fight. If additional clout seems feasible, use a thumb on the spool of a conventional reel or a cupped hand over that of a spinning winch. Employ the classic pumping routine, which will ultimately tire your quarry, and keep the rod tip high so that it will act as a spring to protect a tight line. Exhaust the critter before you steer it beachward.

Beginners often make the major mistake of trying to muscle a fish through inshore breakers. As a result, they part lines or straighten hooks that appeared to be strong enough to conquer giant tuna. Pump the bass shoreward on each cresting wave, but allow it to slide back with the retreating wash. Finally, with proper timing, keep the fish planing on a wave that will deposit it high and reasonably dry. Get down there fast. Grab the leader and slide your catch to a safe location. Never, repeat, *never* try to kick one of these sharp-spined battlers out of the wash. If you do, you may limp for the remainder of the season—we speak from painful experience!

In surf casting from inshore rock piles or jetties it is often impossible to

An autumn morning in New Jersey finds anglers working the surf.

beach a fish in the usual sense of the word, so a long- or short-handled gaff, the length depending on how far one must reach to make contact, becomes a necessity. Paint the handle white so you will be better able to see it after moonset. A gaff can be handy on a sand beach too, particularly where heavy surf makes it difficult to leader-haul a trophy to high ground before it is rescued by an advancing comber. Most of the sand beach regulars prefer a short, stout billy club which will stiffen a bass with a single, sharp whack.

The dangers involved in this sport are slight, although one can get into trouble by remaining on a rock pile or jetty's end after a rising tide prohibits wading ashore. Knock wood, possibly by tapping your headbones, but we have yet to get a hook lodged beyond the barb in any part of personal anatomy. That happens to a lot of people and, usually, is the result of carelessness on one's own part or that of an excited companion. There was a night when we transported an acquaintance into town to see a doctor. The sorrowing lad had unaccountably stuck a big treble hook right through his nose.

It probably will not prove fatal, but there are likely to be some tumbles rarely seen outside of a Japanese gymnasium. Rock piles, slithery with accumulated slime and weed, are not the most stable of casting platforms. Towering breakers, which always arrive when you are not looking thataway, are sneaky. Unless you are alert to their arrival and able to scuttle out of the way or at least turn a braced hip to counter the blow, such waves are figuratively and literally upsetting. Ancient surfmen are great "scuttlers," rivalling sandpipers in this department, but newcomers invariably fail to hear or see a booming comber until they have transcribed a neat loop and landed on their shoulder blades in two or three feet of cold wash. Ice creepers or studded boots are good insurance. The felt soles favored by inland anglers are worthless.

Surfers, no matter how much experience they have logged, seem unable to resist deep wading to reach an offshore bar or attractive rock pile when the tide is close to ebb, but beginning to flood. Since squidding or plugging from such locations can be extremely successful, and because happy hours pass swiftly while the malevolent sea rises, it often becomes necessary to tread water in order to regain shore and complete sanity.

Hal Lyman casting into a New England surf.

There are the usual minor irritations, such as falling asleep on a low beach and awakening to find that a high course tide is doing its best to waft you out to sea; burns suffered by overlong exposure under summer sunlight; and other types of burns—those which raise a white blister on the right thumb or a livid groove in an index finger. The first results from casting hard with a conventional reel prior to wetting the line and thus "lubricating" it; the second when a spincaster gets overly ambitious and leans into a hard cast with too heavy a lure.

Most fishermen are wary of large sharks, yet we cannot recall any striper addict being bitten. Bluefish, beached, flopping, and gnashing their dentures do a much better job of bloodying the careless. One real danger, in addition to a cartwheeling tumble off a jetty or rocky ledge, is too close proximity to a colleague who insists on side-winding his casts. Never a season passes without a few striper enthusiasts cold-caulking friends with tin squids or eel rigs.

When the first edition of this book was published in 1954, we fatuously declared that every wife is impatient with a surf-seduced husband and wont to complain that no hardship ever knocks any sense into his head. That statement dates us, because striper widows are less plentiful now. Many lovelies have become just as eager to wade into the weekend suds as their smitten mates.

Eavesdropping during a recent flaming dawn after a good tide, we heard the tail-end of a conversation between two attractive young women sipping coffee in a sophisticated beach buggy. One was furious. Between gritted teeth she declared, "I wouldn't mind if he only got one, but no—he got *two* without waking me! He can get his own damn breakfast, and if he ever does *that* again I'll divorce the idiot!"

8 · Boats And Bass

STRIPERS BREAKING AND WALLOWING MORE THAN 100 yards offshore are safe from the average shore caster. Add another 50 yards and they are safe from just about anyone other than a skilled veteran using tournament distance tackle. Such fish may cause shore-bound anglers to have a mild apoplexy, to strain shoulder muscles, or to hunt frantically for a lure that will sail 200 yards through the air with line attached. The best solution is a boat to chase bass.

Unlike the surf caster, the boat fisherman is not limited in the area he covers by the distance he can cast a lure. The ocean is all around him and his success is measured only by his ability to find fish, plus his skill in catching them. Indeed, the boatman's options in both methods and gear are almost limitless.

A tremendous amount of area can be covered by the simple process of towing a hook, suitably decorated, behind a craft that is moving over the surface of the sea. Trolling is an age-old method, yet is only a small part of the boatman's repertoire. When occasion demands, he can cast into surfacing schools with any tackle from light surf sticks to fly rods. Jigging, bottom fishing while at anchor, chumming, drift fishing under the influence of currents or winds—together these methods provide bass fishermen with amazing versatility.

Although trolling once was done only by rowers or under sail, since the invention of the internal combustion engine and the subsequent development of the outboard motor, this art has become a science. Boats themselves have changed drastically during the past two decades, both in design and capabilities. Fiberglass has replaced wood to a large extent as a building material, although aluminum holds its own in the construction of small hulls. New space-age developments are likely to spawn additional changes.

At this time diesel fuel for larger craft has been substituted for gasoline. Center consoles have replaced controls at both bow and stern in small boats. Even skiffs have become lighter in weight and easier to handle. Hull designs vary from the typical old high-bow, squat-stern lines of the Harker's Island and Cape Island models to the stable cathedral type that first flourished in the boating market during the early 1950s.

A classic Cuttyhunk bass boat returns to its slip with fish boxes loaded with trophy stripers.

The ardent striped bass fisherman basically considers his boat a platform from which to catch fish. Stability and rugged construction are favored over sleek lines and speed. Leonard "Coot" Hall, who was a living legend in his bassing days around the island of Cuttyhunk off the coast of Massachusetts, put it clearly one evening when we were casting around the rocks of Sow and Pigs Reef at dusk. A huge comber lifted the craft high, then dropped it with a tooth-shaking crunch onto a boulder.

"Don't worry," Coot said calmly. "This is a working boat."

Indeed she was. A two-inch-thick skeg of solid oak had been fastened onto the bottom and run well up the keel to take just this type of abuse. We went on our way without even so much as a started seam.

Choice of hull design, power plant, and size varies not only with a fisherman's taste, but also with the waters in which he plans to seek his quarry. A 32-footer may suit a charter skipper well, since he has to take a payload of at least two anglers on each trip. Such a craft is inefficient and expensive for an individual who specializes in working the sod banks of a tidal marsh. The basic rules are to know the limitations of the boat in question and to take as few chances as possible. Nature, over the course of time, furnishes plenty of unanticipated risks!

Local knowledge of the fishing grounds is vital for any boat fisherman and its importance cannot be over-emphasized. A particular hole may be productive at half-tide but produce nothing at the high or low stages. Bars at tidal river mouths are constantly shifting, and the fish shift with them. Similarly, a sandy bottom in a fast tide rip will change as the force of the water moves the sand one way and another. For the inshore angler, observing bars, holes, banks, and channels at dead-low tide will reveal areas that may hold feeding bass as the water rises. Keeping a log of cross bearings and ranges makes it possible to return to the hot spots at any time.

Both inshore and offshore boatmen should study nautical charts, and the more detailed they are, the better. The National Ocean Survey, which is part of the National Oceanic and Atmospheric Administration under the U. S. Department of Commerce, produces some of the best charts in the world. The navigational information printed on them is obviously valuable for travel from one point to another, but the other, incidental material is of equal importance to fishermen.

Soundings for particular areas, either in fathoms or in feet, are indicated, so that holes and channels may be readily located. The type of bottom is also shown. Thus if stripers are rooting in muddy bottom and suddenly stop hitting, look for similar mud areas in the vicinity, for the school may well have moved on as the food supply was decimated.

Major tide rips are also marked on the charts; these rips are good spots for bass because bait is tumbled out of control and becomes easy prey. Smaller current clashes can be plotted directly on a chart by using elementary piloting procedures or, if well offshore, by the use of a loran. Large underwater boulders and rocks, old wrecks, and similar obstructions are part of the information available on a modern chart. Fish downcurrent from these, for that is where fish lurk.

In brief, charts are a regular spy dossier in detecting striped bass hangouts. They may be purchased directly from outlets of the National Ocean Survey, which is listed in the telephone book under the U. S. Department of Commerce. Most anglers buy them from marine hardware or equipment stores that keep a supply of local charts. Until an angler has memorized his particular fishing grounds thoroughly, these sea-going maps are essential.

Increasingly electronic aids, now considered almost indispensable to boatmen who chase stripers, tilt the scales of fortune. Flashing depth sounders and recording fishfinders read depth and bottom contours and even manage to blip the position of single game fish at varying levels. These advanced "black boxes" are priced well within the budgets of sport fishermen, are compact enough to be installed in small boats, and are so effective that legislation occasionally has been filed to ban their use.

With flasher or recorder, one can literally count down to an otherwise unseen edge or drop-off where bass are dining. Often, when stripers are not spread over an expanse of ground and furiously feeding, they congregate in relatively deep holes where it takes pinpoint accuracy to locate them. A sensitive recording fishfinder bares bassy secrets, showing vulnerable "piles" stacked like pyramids of fishflesh over the bottom. Deep-going lures trolled at the edges or through the centers of such piles usually draw immediate strikes.

Do not disregard any of those tremendously valuable charts that are graced by pencilled x-marks-the-spot notations. Charts are vitally important to accurate navigation along any seacoast. Do copper your bets by using modern electronic sounders that not only locate game fish, but also provide Arguslike eyes for the instant plotting of depth right under your keel. These can be mighty comforting when a helmsman is bewildered in thick fog and begins to wonder whether he is in the channel or merrily cruising toward a fanged rock pile.

Trolling for stripers from boats in the 30-foot class has been popular since the species was first sought by anglers. A close look at this method of fishing will give the basics for any other type of trolling. In the early days, a

Outboard-powered craft are popular among seekers of linesides. In this photo, a Rhode Island middleweight comes aboard a fiberglass hull.

maximum of four lines, known as flat lines, were trailed over the transom. Spoons, bullhead-type feathers, nylons, and bucktails were—and still are— among the favorite lures used. Any of them might be tipped with pork rind or a strip of squid or fish belly to give them more appeal. The four-line limit was simply a practical matter: With more, a hook-up inevitably resulted in massive tangles.

When outriggers became standard equipment on large fishing boats, the number of trolled lines multiplied, for those streamed from an outrigger could be kept clear of the flat lines. Baits or lures on outriggers normally are run on or near the surface because too much weight tends to pull the line free from the clip. A new dimension was added in the early 1970s when downriggers appeared in quantity along the coasts. These devices permit trolling at great depth without excessive strain on rod or line. The weight or vane, which draws the terminal tackle deep, is attached to a separate line by a clip just as the outrigger holds line at the surface. On the strike, the fishing line pulls free and the angler can play the fish without impediment.

Normal trolling tackle for many years consisted of a rather heavy rod with a short, stiff tip. Mounted on this was a reel filled with at least 200 yards of twisted linen 12- to 15-thread line—36- to 45-pound wet test. At the line's terminal end was a swivel, at least two feet of #9 or stronger wire leader, then the lure or bait. To run the lure deep, sinkers ranging up to sash-weight size were added between the line and leader. By today's criteria, anglers were over-gunned for the fish they sought.

Many changes have taken place since those early days. Tackle generally is far lighter, even though some charter skippers lean towards heavy gear simply because newcomers to fishing can break outfits designed for the experienced. Finely braided synthetic lines and monofilament offer less water resistance than the old twisted Cuttyhunk. Lead-core and wire lines run deep without heavy sinkers and the aforementioned downriggers can take braid or mono right to the bottom. The basic techniques, however, have changed little.

If striped bass cannot be spotted breaking the surface, a few straight trolling passes should be made in a locality where they are known to feed. If several lines are out, the quickest method of locating a school is to have each lure riding at a different depth. This system can be applied to all trolling, for there is much logic in covering an area vertically as well as horizontally.

How much line is enough? This is the question asked most often by neophytes. There are many exceptions, but a general figure can be set at 30 yards from rod tip to lure when the boat is traveling at three to five knots over water 20 feet deep. The rule of thumb is to allow five additional yards for every additional foot of depth. With lures like spoons and bucktail-type jigs, the slower the boat goes, the deeper the lures will travel. Conversely, in the case of diving plugs and the like, higher speeds will cause them to run deeper. It pays to change speeds and depths until bass are located.

Spider Andresen prepares to troll deep with the aid of a downrigger. This tool simplifies the streaming of soft lines at any depth.

When an angler really knows the bottom contours under his craft's keel, trolling becomes a fine art. Constant speed should be maintained because sudden changes may spook the fish. As the hull passes over a known hole, pocket, or channel, line is spooled off the reel so that the lure sinks into that depression. Reel gears are then re-engaged, the rod tip is lifted and dropped smartly a couple of times, and chances are good that a striper will grab the hook—a hook that might be ignored if trolled steadily over its hideaway.

When bass are breaking on the surface, gulls and terns are screaming and diving above them, and bait fish shower to escape attack, there is a great temptation for any boat fisherman to head at high speed for the action and to plough through the feeding fish, hoping one or two will grab a trolled hook. This is the worst possible action to take. Speed may be required to get to the general area, but the vessel should then be throttled down to normal trolling speed and the course altered to skirt the school. By running a slightly zigzag path, lures can be made to run in and out of the mass of fish, which may stay surfaced for some time while many of their companions are boated. Frankly, under these conditions, we prefer to kill the motor completely when within casting distance and to toss lures to the bass along the school's edge. Often, however, navigational conditions, other craft in the vicinity, or lack of casting skill among our companions make such a maneuver impossible.

If you are after bass over the 15-pound mark, standard trolling from a large boat changes somewhat from the techniques used for schoolies. These techniques, incidentally, will be discussed when we deal with small craft. Although the same number of flat, outrigger, and downrigger lines may be used, the number should be slanted towards the lower limits, not the higher. A thrashing monster of 40 pounds or more can cause line tangles worthy of a Maltese lacemaker.

Big lures or baits are the rule when trolling for big bass. Among suitable lures on the Atlantic Coast are bunker spoons, which are as large as a hand mirror; plugs that are ten or more inches in length, with swimmers, sub-surface, and deep-running models preferred; and large surgical tubes, often tipped with a sea worm. Eels and eelskin rigs, often with a variety of lead-heads or wobble-plates added, are favorites after dark. Among natural baits, whole menhaden, mackerel, herring, and squid lead the field.

On the Pacific side, spoons and metal jigs are favored, along with the Japanese fixed-hook feather jig. In Oregon, the old tuna bone jig of Hawaiian ancestry is also used successfully. Plugs also produce, but eels and eelskin rigs seem to be ignored by western bass, undoubtedly because there are no eels of this type in Pacific waters and the fish are not accustomed to dining on them. Although sardines, anchovies, sculpins—known locally as bullheads—and squid are used widely by Pacific anglers when still fishing, live-lining, or drifting, none has ever become popular as a trolling bait. Throughout the entire San Francisco Bay area, anglers tend to troll when stripers are feeding on small fish and when the water is comparatively clear.

The umbrella lure, which is really a whole group of lures, can also be a killer of big bass. We, and a host of charter captains, hate to use this rig because it is as difficult to handle as an angry giraffe. Even when only one fish is hooked, the tangles and flying hooks as the striper is boated endanger anyone within range. If two fish are hooked simultaneously—and this often happens—hooks can end up embedded in human flesh.

Although straight trolling will take bass, imparting action to the lure or bait by jigging—lifting the rod tip smartly and letting it drop back again at regular intervals—will bring better results. This is particulary true when using lures, such as the bucktail types, that have no built-in action of their own. Extra action may also be imparted by changing the boat's course or by changing speed. Abrupt speed changes should be avoided, however, for the difference in propeller noise may spook the fish or at least make them more wary.

Twenty years ago, #9 or #12 stainless steel wire was the standard leader material for seeking big stripers. A swivel connected the wire to the line, at which point sinkers were added to make the hook run deep. The terminal end of the wire was either twisted into the lure or hook eye, or fastened with a snap swivel. Today, heavy monofilament has taken over to a large extent. Forty-pound test is preferred, with fifty-pound running a close second. Anything heavier than that can be seen too readily by bass, particularly in clear water. When toothed species like bluefish are in the same waters as bass, we choose nylon-covered cable-wire leaders because they are easier to handle than stainless steel, have no appreciable glitter, and do not kink. The snap swivel has fallen from grace in most bassing waters because it impairs the action of the lure. It has been replaced by a simple snap, or the lure is tied directly to the leader.

The length of the leader should be about three feet. Some anglers go as high as ten with mono. There are two reasons for a long leader: First, a big bass thrashing alongside a boat can cut the line just before it is gaffed or netted; second, a long leader makes a large lure ride more evenly but with maximum action. The deception factor must also be considered, although if you are using monofilament line or are fishing at night, this factor is minimal.

The fundamental connection between fish and fisherman is the hook. When hooks are an integral part of a lure, as is the case with a plug, they should be of heavy or extra-heavy wire. Big stripers can crunch a hard-shelled clam like popcorn and will do the same with light hooks. The O'Shaughnessy style is favored in sizes 2/0 and 4/0 for school bass and 6/0 to 8/0 for cows. However, the Pacific Coast Siwash is actually a better trolling hook. It has a needle point, which must be kept sharpened, and a deep bite, which makes for immediate penetration and good holding qualities. It is not inclined to tear flesh or to "buttonhole."

Once a large fish has been hooked, the boat should be stopped or headed into wind or current at idling speed so that it is comparatively motionless.

Stripers hitting a trolled lure usually hook themselves, but few will hook themselves so solidly that they can be dragged astern in the last stages of the battle without breaking loose. To prevent fouled lines, all lures except the one wearing the bass should be reeled aboard. Often another fish will hit during this reeling-in process, so take care that all is ready for the added action.

In playing a striped bass, whether from a small boat or a large one, the most dangerous moment is when the leader appears above the water. At this instant, many a "dead" fish comes to life, thrashes on the surface, or dives under the keel to break free. Never increase the reel drag as the striper becomes exhausted. A fairly light drag, aided by the human thumb on the reel spool, is the best insurance available as you pump the lineside into close quarters.

Virginia's Chesapeake Bay Bridge Tunnel plays host to vast schools of stripers in the fall. Here, boatmen maneuver close to the barnacle-encrusted pilings.

If the fish does dive under the keel, do not hesitate to dip the rod tip deep in the water while maintaining tension. The arc of the rod, now underwater rather than in the air, normally will guide the line clear. Needless to say, this is not the time to relax your grip on the butt!

Bringing a fish aboard is a technique in itself. On a charter boat, the skipper or mate will grasp the leader with a gloved hand and swing gaff or net into action. If the fish is to be kept, aim the gaff for the head and shoulder area; if to be released, try to get the gaff point under the lower jaw—often a difficult job—or swing it aboard with the leader. When netting, hold the net stationary in the water and lead the bass head-first into the net bag before lifting it. Waving the mesh around like a butterfly-catcher is not recommended. If you are fishing without benefit of a mate, guide the striper towards the boat's side by swinging the rod at an angle of not more than 20 degrees above the horizontal. In their excitement, neophytes are apt to lift the rod tip straight to the sky. The result—a broken rod, a parted line, a lost bass, or a combination of all three.

Trolling, as anyone who has seen the Weweantic River in Massachusetts or the waters off China Camp in California's San Pablo Bay during the striper runs knows, is not confined to big boats. Craft, ranging from car-top types to the center console models previously mentioned, are powered for the most part by outboard or inboard-outboard motors. Selection depends upon the water to be fished, the taste of the angler, and, perhaps most importantly, the depth of his pocketbook.

However, even small boats propelled by oars take their share of bass. Before the days of gasoline engines, an angler in a rowboat broke all records, and all hands have been trying to duplicate the trick ever since. Charles B. Church, fishing with an eel at Quick's Hole between Nashawena and Pasque islands off the Massachusetts coast, on August 17, 1913, hooked and boated a 73-pound striped bass that stood as, first an official, and then an unofficial rod-and-reel world record until 1981.

Many claim, and we are among them, that the noise of an outboard or any other engine will, under certain conditions, drive bass away or make them so suspicious of a trolled lure that they will not hit. This is particularly true when the bottom contour is rocky with many deep caverns, in which propeller noise apparently reverberates. In such circumstances, kill the motor and resort to an ash breeze for propulsion.

As is true for any statement in bass fishing, one should never say always. At times, propeller turbulence appears to stir up and even attract stripers. Fishing off Maryland's Eastern Shore near Crisfield years ago, Captain Alex Kellam, the embodiment of the Chesapeake Bay waterman, illustrated this to us clearly. School fish were all over the place and we were casting for them without success. Alex started the motor, we trolled with a long line over the muddy bottom between clumps of marsh grass and hooked fish with reg-

Twelve- to fourteen-foot small boats are still manhandled into mild surf. One man manages the oars while another pushes off, then leaps aboard and fires up the outboard motor.

ularity. Alex's explanation was that the mud had been stirred up, liberating all sorts of the goodies upon which bass feed; the schoolies swam over to investigate and arrived just in time to see a tasty lure passing overhead. This theory produced results and we cannot quarrel with it.

Along the New England coast in particular, one of the favored methods of taking bass from a small boat is with sea worm and spinner. The spinner is placed at least a foot ahead of the worm, which should be affixed to the hook so that it streams naturally. This combination, fished early and late in the season, night or day, is a killer of school stripers and has accounted for a few large specimens as well.

Inlets, bays, and tidal rivers provide the best grounds for this type of trolling, but remember that it pays to play the edges of a channel or the drop-off near shore. In a deep-running river, bait and attractor should be trolled as near the bank as it is possible to troll safely. Bass feed among the grass and rushes that grow in such areas, so the closer you get to them, the better. If you lack sea worms, plastic replicas or a thin strip of squid or fish belly can be substituted.

Trolling speed in a small boat varies little from that used with larger craft. Moving at three to four knots for cows and four to five knots for school stripers is a good general rule. An outboard has an advantage since it is more maneuverable. If a strike is missed at a given spot, the boat may be turned fairly quickly, run back on a course parallel to the original one and at least ten yards from it, and turned again so that the lure is presented in exactly the same manner over the pay-off waters. In general, it is a mistake to reverse

Larger, center-console bass boats are now launched into the surf with the aid of a prime mover, usually a four-wheel-drive "chase car."

course and follow a path that brings the lure over the strike area in a direction opposite from the original one. Stripers normally lie with their heads upcurrent and, as both boat and line pass over them before the lure is within striking distance, they may be spooked.

No matter what the boat size, a knowing skipper trolls so that the lure passes over good water even though the hull may not. Thus, in a tide rip, the course will be set to carry the hook across the edge of the rip itself, while the craft's keel may be many yards from the current clash. Similarly, trolling across an inlet or river mouth at an angle will produce more fish than will steering straight up- or downcurrent. By changing course sharply, the line may be made to pass over a spot that cannot be reached by the boat itself.

Such trolling tricks are the result of experience. There are some, however, that can be learned before putting out to sea. One of these, previously mentioned, is pumping or jigging the lure by raising and lowering the rod tip. If a swirl, indicating a short strike, is seen, the working of the lure often will bring bass to hook. If it does not, the reel drag can be slackened so that the bait drops astern and downward. When the drag is tightened again, the lure darts forward. Skilled anglers achieve the same effect by putting the reel into free-spool, keeping a restraining thumb on the line, then engaging the gears again. Do not try this unless you are completely familiar with your tackle; you will have the mother of all backlashes if a bass hits when the drag is disengaged.

Many anglers wonder why they often score a strike just after the boat has made a turn. The answer is simple: The lure not only changes direction, it also changes speed and depth. Of course, the only way to change direction is to alter the course of the boat itself. Many skippers do just that by steering a gentle zigzag course. Variations in speed and therefore in depth can be initiated by way of the throttle, but it is preferable for the most part to accomplish this by pumping the rod or by alternately reeling and slackening the line. However, do not be afraid to change your base speed when strikes are few and far between.

A high vantage point makes a great deal of difference to the boat fisherman who is trying to locate bass. Within reasonable safety limits, standing at the highest point on the craft will help you to get a bird's-eye view of what goes on beneath the surface. When conditions are good and the water clear and calm, stripers may be spotted many feet below the surface. Polarized glasses help greatly in such scouting. Binoculars also are of benefit for watching either birds or fellow anglers at a distance.

A school of fish may travel at a high rate of speed or they may sound. To pinpoint the spot where the fish have been is easy enough if there are plenty of landmarks to determine cross bearings. Usually, however, such landmarks are scarce when they are most needed. Small dye markers, fish oil, or even a bit of newspaper can be tossed over the side to mark the area. We used to suggest a rag soaked in lube oil for this purpose, but pollution-conscious Coast Guardsmen take a dim view of such activity!

The best way to take surfacing striped bass from a boat is to stop forward motion entirely and then, using a light rod, to cast into the school. This system has been developed to a fine art along certain sections of the coasts and is used whether the fish are visible or not. So specialized has it become that a particular type of craft known as a bass boat has been developed.

Originating off the Sandy Hook area of New Jersey, moving from there to Long Island's Montauk, thence to Cuttyhunk Island and the Elizabeth Islands chain in Massachusetts, bass boat fishing has spread to some degree along all coasts. The original design was of extremely rugged lapstrake construction measuring anywhere from 14 to 25 feet, with the most common in the 16- to 22-foot bracket. The inboard power plant was large for the hull, a safety factor as well as a convenience when speeding from one hot spot to another. Dual controls for the engine and tillers located fore and aft ensured quick maneuvering under all conditions. An open cockpit, although wet in

A center-console Boston Whaler heads at full throttle for the shore, where it will touch down and slide well up onto the sand beach.

heavy weather, was a prime feature allowing casting to cover a 360-degree range. Many such craft are still being built, although most are now powered by outboards.

Bass boats of this type can endure almost anything coastal waters offer, and often must do so. The warning hiss of a comber about to break at the crest is familiar music to the striper skipper playing the beach edge. He depends upon his engine and hull to get him out of there, fast, before the wave breaks, or to get him out of there, somehow, after it does. A self-bailing cockpit is a necessity. This type of angling offers some of the most exciting sport on a striper fisherman's schedule but is best left to experts.

Long casts are neither required nor desired. For this reason, a regular surf rod is a nuisance, chiefly because the long butt is awkward to handle in the close confines of a cockpit. Choose a rod with a butt length of 18 to 20 inches, with a comparatively short tip and plenty of backbone. Often a fish must be horsed away from a sheltering, line-breaking rock or be lost for sure. Light tackle can mean dropped fish and vanished terminal rigs.

Often boat casting may be combined with trolling. A fisherman who tosses a plug shoreward from the bow as one or two of his companions troll astern with sub-surface lures, not only helps to locate bass, but also brings them more readily to the trolled hook. A striper often follows a cast offering right up to the boat, swirls at it, sounds, and then takes a trolled lure as it passes a few seconds later.

Non-fishermen often chuckle over the image of a beach caster wading deep into the surf and throwing a lure with all his might so that it will reach a spot where a boat is passing. On the boat, another caster puts equal effort into the task of tossing his lure as close as possible to the beach. For reasons best known to the bass, a plug, jig, or eel swimming away from the beach towards open water has more appeal then the same tempter heading shoreward. This fact makes boat casting a very effective method of taking fish.

Such a method is not confined to the regular bass boat. More and more anglers are discovering that a lure thrown into the water from any kind of floating vehicle produces as well as or better than the same lure trolled. In addition, spots that are inaccessible to a trolled line can be reached readily by casting. This holds true particularly in estuarine areas where small outboard-powered craft are at peak efficiency. Light tackle has given this game an additional shot in the arm, for the sea-going baitcasting rod or spinning outfit are ideal weapons for this work. Fly-fishing tackle is also excellent for presenting small lures in very shallow water without spooking the stripers.

Many one-time surf-casting purists have now taken to boats. Initially, back in the late 1940s, adventurous mechanized anglers favored 12- to 14-foot car-top skiffs made of plywood, aluminum or fiberglass fitted with small- to medium-sized outboard motors and oars. After the mid-1960s craft with fiberglass hulls of 16 to 22 feet, powered by big outboards, increasingly pleased latter-day corsairs. Beautifully rigged and equipped with the latest in navigational aids, these dune-based fishing machines are far too heavy for manhandling, so four-wheel-drive beach buggies must be used to push them into the breaking waves and to ensure recovery after full-power landings. Needless to say, trailers are essential for this sort of boating.

Canvas-covered boats have been used, but they are not rugged enough to stand the punishment on rocky or even pebbly beaches. The larger craft are far easier to launch and recover, with a prime mover, than are the light, car-top skiffs now largely relegated to ancient history. However, once launched in the surf—a dangerous practice for any but experienced hands—any reasonably seaworthy hull and power plant combination will take a caster out beyond the breakers to the vicinity of offshore bars and rips. Surf boats are used variously for trolling, as casting platforms, for drift fishing, or for live-lining at anchor.

It should be noted that artificial lures are not the only bass-takers cast from boats of all kinds. The rigged eel and eelskin are among the items that were used for enticing stripers in the early days, but now almost anything goes. A live or dead menhaden, herring, mackerel, squid, or sardine may be lobbed into a school of feeding fish or in the general direction of a spot where bass are known to lurk. We use the word "lobbed" advisedly. If a snap cast is used, the bait will part company from the hook and, if a monster striper then comes up and swallows it, suicide may seem a welcome alternative to frustration.

Spinning was oversold to many salt water anglers when it first became popular in this country after World War II. Then it was not unusual to see boat fishermen trolling happily with this type of tackle, which is designed primarily for casting. If it is the only outfit on hand, naturally it will do. However, if there is any choice, the free-spool reel and matching rod should be used when trolling. These provide better control of the line, lure, or bait, and also of the bass when playing it. At times it becomes necessary to put heavy pressure on a fish to keep it away from underwater obstructions, and the conventional outfit is best suited to "persuade" in a barroom brawl.

Immediately after World War II, wire line began to invade the striper coasts. Universally frowned upon as unsporting at the outset, metal strands are now cheerfully accepted and employed on everything from school bass in the shallows to potential trophies feeding on deep-down bottom structures. Since wire lining has just about evolved into a separate trolling discipline, we examine its credentials in a following chapter.

In any type of boat fishing, there are signs that indicate bass are near, and knowledge of these signs helps to make a trip successful. The most common indicators are sea birds. A wheeling, screaming cloud of them, dipping and plunging above frantic bait, warms the heart of any striper man. A pair of binoculars will assist in identification. On our Pacific side, Bonaparte's gulls are most commonly seen over bass schools. Atlantic anglers are most likely to see herring, black-backed gulls and, from New Jersey northward, terns. As the sport moves south laughing gulls replace terns as aerial spotters.

Often the fish under bait schools cannot be seen breaking. Obviously, if the striped sides and dark back of a striper can be distinguished as they make a surface attack on forage, all questions are answered. Certainly a knowledge of the habits of other species on the grounds can save a mad dash to the scene of a presumed watery victory. For example, bluefish tend to leave dead and dying bait on the surface, while stripers take their meals whole. Bonito and other members of the tuna clan normally break water when feeding and can be identified. Mackerel ruffle the surface, but without great disturbance—and so on.

Experience is the best teacher. Lacking that, catching a fish from whatever school is encountered provides positive proof. Note also that birds, particularly the larger gulls, will feed upon just about anything, so beware of chasing the wake of a garbage scow or speeding to an area where a commercial fisherman has just hauled nets.

Sometimes it may seem to the uninitiated that an experienced skipper is relying on his sense of smell for navigation as well as for locating fish. This is particularly true at night, a time when bass are apt to be feeding heartily, and it is then that local knowledge pays off to the fullest. One of Cuttyhunk's most famous guides said that "summer fishermen" can always be distinguished from native experts after sundown. Only the natives remain on the rips near the rocky, dangerous grounds after dark. Visitors, lacking experienced guides, wisely scurry for port.

Oddly enough, a dark lure often gets best results at night. Black plugs, deep-colored nylons, bucktails and feathers, ancient and graying eels outfish lighter lures. As for luminous types—not the mildly fluorescent, but the ones that glow under their own power—we have found them practically worthless. When Nature illuminates line, leader, and lure with phosphorescence, many trollers head for home. Fish can be taken under these conditions, but the angler has to work harder for each catch. Fine monofilament line, a metal lure that has built-in, fast action, and a swift current sometimes can beat that accursed "fire in the water," and brilliant moonlight also may help to defeat it.

Whether fishing at night or during the day from a boat of any sort, there are a few things to remember that have to do with the sea, safety, and courtesy rather than with actual fishing. Coast Guard-approved life jackets must be carried for every passenger aboard. After sundown, proper lights must be displayed and, aboard most powered craft, day and night flares are also required. Add a sound signalling device and a compass if you plan to reach home without swimming. If you have a radio telephone, remember that it is a communications device, not a gossip circuit.

Cutting just ahead or astern of a fellow troller is not only unmannerly, it is often construed as an unofficial declaration of war. By the same token, speeding through another angler's chum slick is a prelude to mayhem. Pressing close to a beach where casters are fishing may well result in a shower of tinclads on deck—or head. In brief, common courtesy means better fishing for all concerned.

9 · Wire A Bass

METAL FISHING LINES, LIKE SO MANY OTHER AIDS TO marine angling, originated on inland waters where trollers sought lake trout and other deep feeders with spoons and bait-spinner combinations. It is likely that sport and commercial harvesters of the Great Lakes were first to experiment with soft-drawn copper strand in the 1930s, after which there was swift acceptance of wire by sportsmen throughout hinterland America. Quite naturally, success in the taking of inland salmonoids intrigued fishers of the sea. Immediately after World War II, heavy Monel was taking considerable numbers of king mackerel from grounds off the southern United States.

This was a handlining operation, abhorrent to a great many classicists, so metal's salty debut drew a chorus of Bronx cheers from all but commercially oriented watermen. Now well established, wire lining is still held in low repute by a dwindling percentage of citizens, but, properly employed, the strand is quite as sporting as any other line. Deep-going metal helps to deck tons of striped bass annually.

For various reasons, wire was little used by sport fishermen prior to the late 1940s. Acceptance came after wartime research had advanced metallurgy and as a result of a boom in the development of seaworthy small boats. Prior to that time, most striper fishing enthusiasts relied on tender skiffs and the ash breeze to present trolled lures or baits in sheltered waters. "Deep-going" meant no more than prospecting a fathom or two, a depth that could be plumbed with soft lines and light sinkers. New needs dictated new equipment and, as usual, bright seafarers quickly adapted inland techniques to solve marine problems. They learned early on that wiring can be highly productive and highly demanding.

Wire can be as light as desired, which in turn means that diameters and pound-test brackets are best chosen for specific tasks. Wire is effective in both shallow and deep water, and there is no overkill. In addition, a bass hooked on metal seems to fight much harder than one played on soft line. This, of course, is due to metal's lack of stretch; it has none of the forgiving angler-aiding elasticity of nylon monofilament or braids. Aside from the resilience of your rod and the adjustment of your reel drag, you are tied in solid.

As a rule of thumb, 20-pound-test may be considered "light," but there is need for 30 and 45. Test choice is not determined solely by the weight of the fish sought, but by other considerations. These include the intended fishing depth, manipulation of a given lure, and the water resistance of certain tempters, such as the spreader rig called an "umbrella" or—a term swiftly disappearing in modern jargon—a "Christmas tree."

What about the supposed handicapping weight of metal so often cited by detractors? This is a matter of comparative nitpicking. Striped bass are not habitual jumpers, but many of the more acrobatic species taken on light- to medium-weight metal rocket skyward with the greatest of ease.

The fact that wire is nearly unforgiving, especially when it is made of single-strand steel or Monel, nobody will deny. The springy stuff regularly destroys egotism during that initial act of "streaming" a lure or bait, and be assured that nothing under the sea wind is so thoroughly tangled and difficult to correct as a wire line backlash! Single-strand wire, in the hands of inexperienced folk, also welcomes the slightest opportunity to kink. When this happens, usually after a miniscule loop is allowed to snug up, the metal crystallizes at that point and parts under even slight tension. Any kink must be studiously avoided, for it is far more debilitating than the "wind knot" thrown into a tapered leader while fly casting. Beginners go red in the face when impossible snarls develop during inept streaming, and people briefly consider jumping overboard when a lengthy hank of persnickety metal wraps itself around the lower unit of an outboard motor.

The art of streaming wire line will not be learned by any perusal of the literature, for that skill comes only with experience. Masters of the technique are rarely embarrassed, since they observe a step-by-step routine which appears effortless, much like the upland gunner's apparently instantaneous "snap shot," in which a bird is tumbled with no evident lead or swing-through. The fact that elementary rules of physics always apply is lost on the casual observer.

Single-strand wire, among its other mind-boggling tricks, is springy and quick to overrun when poorly controlled. Hence, one must follow a procedure. First, maintaining constant click-ratchet drag or using a strong and educated thumb, drop a lure over the side and carefully feed it back into the boat's wake. Allow line to depart from the reel slowly, speeding the operation only when the lure begins to bite into the water and provide line tension. Often a click drag is not sufficient to prevent overrun without additional thumb pressure, but the danger of fluffing and the consequent backlash diminishes with each additional yard between reel spool and lure. It looks easy in the hands of an expert, but this dropback can be a major hurdle for a tyro.

Strip a yard or two at a time until the line gradually tightens, maintaining control until such time as the lure has reached the planned strike zone and the clutch may be engaged. Only then disengage the click-ratchet; otherwise a

Typical wire-line reels and a rod equipped with roller guides. Metal reel spools are favored in this work, and roller guides are the most efficient in playing fish.

striper's powerful run following its savage strike will raise a shriek like a hacksaw ripping through a tin can.

Do not, in essaying this opening gambit, fatuously attempt to emulate the experienced small-boat skipper's use of thumb pressure alone on a revolving spool and his sang-froid in streaming wire at full throttle. The man *is* proceeding step by step, although he has the routine mastered to the point of oiled efficiency. Nobody cracks the throttle wide open until proper line tension has been assured. However, a well-trained helmsman increases speed very rapidly until the proper line marking races through rod guides, the throttle is chopped, and the boat slams down off plane to pursue a more leisurely fishing pace. Nobody is likely to witness high-speed streaming aboard a charter vessel, simply because the skipper knows that some of his bookings cannot handle the technique.

Favored wire types are relatively few in number. Striped bass fishermen still catch the odd lineside on soft-drawn copper, but this metal is no longer of importance since it lacks the strength of stainless steel or Monel, is larger in diameter per pound test, and tends to corrode in salt water. Practically all of today's bassing bets are placed on single-strand steel, Monel, or lead-core braid. Lead-core braid is simply a sheath of soft multifilament (a Chinese finger-trap) with a slim core of plebian lead.

There is limited use of twisted and loose-braided steel, neither of which in our opinion has much to recommend it other than resistance to kinking and somewhat greater ease of handling. Both are larger in diameter than comparable single-strand wire, and they are susceptible to fraying when dragged over a rough bottom. They also are abrasive to rod guides.

Lead-core is easiest for a beginner to control; hence it often adorns the reels of charter skippers whose patrons may well be sampling sea sport for the first time. Since the line is soft and malleable there is less danger of backlashing in the process of streaming. Kinks do not have to be so scrupulously avoided, because the nylon sheath retains its strength even when its lead core is fractured. This type of line almost always is color-coded by intervals, so that the length trolled is easily determined during daylight hours. Fishermen on the grounds tend to be laconic, but an unsuccessful bloke will know precisely what is meant when a more fortunate acquaintance shouts across the waves, "Four colors!" or whatever he happens to be sending out and down to pay-off territory.

Lead-core, in addition to its greater bulk and slower decent, also has an exasperating habit of molding itself around bottom obstructions when slacked off. If one of the inevitable hangups occurs while you are dredging deep pastures, by all means keep a taut line while backing down. Otherwise the irritating strand will embrace, partially encircle, and cling to every boulder in its path. Connections between leader and line or line and backing create no difficulty here, for knots used to join nylon monofilament or nylon and braided dacron suffice. It is necessary to use different connections in attaching straight wire to softer backing.

The methods vary, although each joint is calculated to ensure strength as well as smooth passage through rod guides. Generally, the forward end of the backing line is looped, using a Surgeon's Knot or sometimes as simple a thing as a Spider Hitch. The Spider Hitch tests a fraction under 100 percent and is far easier to construct than the much-touted Bimini Twist. In joining wire to braid, pass the tag-end of the metal through the soft loop, allowing at least 18 inches of wire to overlap. Make seven turns around both standing parts of the braid, and then wrap back toward the initial juncture. Finish with several tight twists of wire.

Where metal is jury-rigged into a loop of braided backing, *sans* the shock-absorbing twists, there is some danger of cutting the soft material. Therefore, in such "quickie" joints, double-wrap the loop around the smooth eye of wire. Some capable trollers prefer barrel swivels as connections. These must be small enough to rattle through the guides without jamming, and they serve as an audible warning on a dark night.

Single-strand wire, like all wire, should be marked with waterproof enamel or ink dye at predetermined points, say every 50 feet, or with whatever reminders appear necessary on a chosen ground. We suggest for all-around operation markers at 50, 100, 150, 200, and 300 feet; it is not difficult to interpolate between or beyond these. Color-coding is helpful, yet some measure of "feel" must be built in for nighttime trolling. This can be achieved by using a single tight wrapping of dental floss or one-eighth-inch wide waterproof plastic stripping tape at the initial reference point, two circlets at the second, and so on. Proper marking can be done on a temporarily vacant football field, either by pacing off approximate measurements or by employing a steel tape measure.

If a leader is deemed essential, it is most often joined to running wire via a barrel swivel and a well-made Haywire Twist and to a terminal hook or lure by some other means. Wire often is connected directly to a trolled offering by way of a practical stainless steel locking snap. Have nothing to do with archaic, angular, trouble-prone, safety-pin snaps.

Do not skimp on backing! Pack as much as possible under a shot of wire and insist upon dacron braid that is of a heavier pound test rating than up-front steel. Dacron's stretch is slight and it does not possess the destructive "memory" of nylon monofilament. Mono, until physicists get around to rearranging its molecular structure so that it will not revert to its original diameter after stretching under pressure, is a poor choice for this office.

Immediately discard any notion that wire line can be used with a spinning reel, for in spite of the fixed-spool's versatility, it cannot work with metal on a trolling ground. There, the conventional reel occupies a niche of its own, one that is unlikely to be challenged in a foreseeable future. One still enjoys a large choice of revolving-spool winches that vary in size from the big 4/0 down to the relatively miniature bay and plug casting models. Perhaps an ideal all-purpose wire-line reel simply has yet to be invented, since so many currently available types meet the basic requirements. Narrow-spool classics, like the Penn Mariner, help to prevent overrun and ease line-laying in retrieve, but enthusiasts normally place their faith in standard offshore trolling designs. Line-levelling devices are highly efficient here, but many regulars trust their agile right thumbs to keep their spools smoothly packed and level from bell to bell.

Any reel selected for wiring should be ruggedly constructed and fitted with an easily adjusted drag mechanism, plus free-spool and workhorse gearing. Retrieve ratios range from 2½ to 1 for normal trolling, although there is considerable interest in 5 to 1. This last offers no demonstrated benefit other than rapid bring-back of a lure that must be cleared of fouling weed. Many members of the surf-casting fraternity who sally offshore in small boats succeed with the typical wide-spooled squidding reels. Where wire is chosen, however, tough metal spools are far superior to any of the featherweight casting types.

Single-action fly-casting reels are unlikely tools offshore, but they do see limited service in estuaries, river systems, and quiet bays. Most of these line-storers lack anything more restraining than a light click drag and they are best mounted on a big fly-casting blank which, unlike a majority of long wands employed by classic feather merchants, is equipped with Carbaloy ring guides to allow smooth line passage and resist the abrasive caresses of wire. Since a fly rod is resilient, there is no compelling reason to fit a roller tip top, something considered necessary on even the lightest of offshore trolling sticks designed to handle metal.

Here, more so than in trolling with soft line, roller guides provide a distinct advantage. At the very least, except on a modified fly rod, fit a roller tip top. Unless one develops bad habits and cants the rod sharply while playing a bass, line-cutting grooves will not develop. Canting will certainly groove a roller guide's bridge and, sooner or later, the wire is sure to hop off its smoothly spinning saddle and jam in the jagged cut.

Wire is tough, yet it should be given proper maintenance. Crystallization is a constant foe with single-strand, most often made apparent by a sudden parting at the point where a kink has weakened the molecular structure, or where continuous jigging has caused deterioration through flexing at the tip top. Metal deteriorates with use in any case and an educated thumb can feel it becoming progressively harder and therefore more brittle. There is no repair, no cure other than replacement of the entire strand when the danger signals appear. Frustration is likely if one starts a new season with last year's wire.

Maintenance, in addition to discarding any questionable line, consists of constant vigilance, first to detect apparently insignificant loops and to straighten them before they snug up to become dangerous kinks. If mild straightening is impossible, it is better to cut the wire at the critical location and splice it. Lay the two ends together, facing each other; wrap each seven or eight turns over the other, and finish with Haywire Twists fore and aft. Single-strand Monel or stainless steel wire also profits by being washed after the day's fishing with clean fresh water to flush out the accumulated salts.

Since a line will progressively weaken at that point where it flexes over a rod's tip top in jigging, there are two ways to ensure virgin strength. If only part of a standing line is streamed, learn to pay out or retrieve a foot or so of it at regular intervals, thus eliminating a single stress point. Better yet, use just enough wire to extend from the transom to the strike zone, after which go a foot or more into the braided backing where flex is no threat.

There is no all-purpose rod made for wire-line trolling. They range from light, fairly resilient models designed to handle fine metal up to approximately 50-pound-class sticks for heavier work. Standard lengths, ranging from the usual offshore 6½ feet to 7 feet overall, are ideal. Butt sections, from the rubber cap or gimbal nock to reel position, seem most comfortable when they are within the 18- to 24-inch bracket. Even where a very light stick is employed, the extension butt is an aid.

In general, striped bass fishing is a stand-up sport. Where big fish are likely to be found, a belt socket can be helpful, but there is no need to don a shoulder or kidney harness. In order to maintain reasonable cockpit discipline, charter skippers like portable fishing chairs, some of which are fitted with gimbals, but more of which are facsimiles of ordinary lawn chairs with rubber-capped, deck-hugging legs. It is possible to stream more than two lines off a transom, but twins are safest where tangles must be avoided. In small boat operations it is customary for one angler to work a lure from the port side, while the other streams from starboard.

Chairs provide a measure of comfort in loppy seaways, particularly for landlubbers who have yet to acquire their sea legs and for the inevitable victim of *mal de mer*. Never scoff at this latter affliction, for the hardiest of offshore types occasionally succumbs. We chuckle now in recalling a screaming black night off Cuttyhunk with Captain Bob Smith, when a deck chair would surely have appealed to Kib Bramhall.

We left the slip when "we should have stood in bed." Famed Quick's Hole was a crashing maelstrom and it was alive with trophy bass. Those of us aboard were using wire, sub-surface swimming plugs, and the old Russel-lures, which apparently have never been consistent winners on any bass ground other than Vineyard Sound. Bramhall, who is one of America's great painters, and who also is well versed in every method used to tweak stripers out of the sea, contracted a rare case of *mal de mer*.

We offered no sympathy. One of us, having just boated a 40-pounder, commanded, "You might as well put that chum to good use. Grab my chair and catch a bass between gulps!"

He complied—and streamed no more than 50 feet of metal before a 60-pounder inhaled the bug!

Tackle was beefed up that night: fairly stiff trolling rods and conventional reels filled with 200 yards of heavy backing topped off with 100-foot shots of 45-pound-test stainless steel. Our skipper had zeroed in on his target area and, until he figured that we were competent, advised streaming exactly 23 "pulls of line." This means, against a click-ratchet's resistance, 23 arm-length strips off the reel's spool. Bob's bass boat jockeyed into position upcurrent of the rip's boiling face and he knew that lures paid out properly would swing right into the strike zone.

The length of line trolled is always dictated by the immediate need. An average might be 120 feet, yet this may be shortened to good advantage when the stripers are aggressive and the water is deep enough to prevent undue spooking by a vessel's passage. At the other extreme, there is nothing horrendous about paying out some of the backing.

With notable exceptions, one rarely needs more than the 100 yards packed on an over-the-counter spool. Actually, a common error is to drag more wire than is required for best results. However, the correct length is dependent on several factors, such as the depth to be plumbed, strand type,

Warren Williams, Jr., using wire and a large, narrow-spooled reel, gaffs a striper that hit a deep-going, plastic-dressed leadhead.

test and consequent weight, length to be streamed, the force of the current, and the design and heft of a given lure. Add your actual over-the-ground boat speed and the equation gets a mite complicated.

There are rules of thumb in trolling. Usually lines, if more than one go into the wake, should be at roughly equal distances from each other on the transom. This helps to prevent tangling and also creates the illusion in the water of "a school of bait." Do not make sharp turns, for these invariably cause a slackening of line tension with the result that the lures plunge bottomward and are fouled. Check your boat speed with an eye to the wind and current flow, noting that there are considerable differences in progress when one is cruising up, down, or across moving water. Keep in mind also that bass are most likely to feed avidly in moving water; hence slack ebb or flood are less likely to produce strikes than conditions in between.

Skippers work the big rips in different ways, often positioning their vessels just ahead of a clashing face and allowing the lures to swing down and into the turbulence. When capable helmsmen work together, it is not difficult to hold position until a fish is hooked, then to move forward until the gaff is planted. The boat may then be backed down into its mutually accepted slot.

One highly productive and gentler technique was evolved by inland wet fly fishermen. A troller steams downcurrent toward a rip, streaming a proper length of line. The vessel is turned to port or starboard just far enough in front of the rip's face so that the lure will swim down and across that point where the bass are assumed to be lined up, waiting for flustered bait to be swept into their chow line.

Deep jigging is usually defined as allowing a heavy lure to plummet almost vertically, after which it is jigged just above the bottom rubble or brought back toward the surface in a series of sharp up-and-down motions. However, there is much need for another breed of jigging in straight wire-line trolling with such lures as lead-heads, which possess no built-in action. This is an acquired art, fatiguing until an angler develops easy rhythm. It consists of a regular sharp pulse forward of no more than a foot or so, followed by a dropback of the same distance. This may result from an up-and-down motion of the rod tip, which is hard on the arm muscles and rarely so productive as a nearly horizontal, metronome-like sway in which the arms, shoulders, and back share the strain. After a while, however, the motion becomes nearly automatic and, once mastered, is far from muscle-busting. Invariably, strikes are scored on that short dropback after a lure is given forward motion.

Either natural baits or artificial lures can be used to advantage, yet trollers have developed a preference for lead-head jigs, swimming plugs, spoons, and tube lures, including the spreader-rigged umbrella. The latter can be deadly on daylight tides, since, with four or more surgical tubes of various colors radiating out from a central hub plus a centrally fixed artificial, it looks like a school of bait. Each of these lures is armed, so that the umbrella becomes a potentially dangerous weapon at boatside or when a thrashing striper is swung aboard. Spreaders are relatively heavy and present considerable water resistance, so tackle must be beefed up to the 45- or 50-pound-test class. Unfortunately, in addition to catching bass, spreaders maim a percentage of them because of their overabundance of swinging hooks.

A majority of the plugs used by wire-liners are sub-surface swimming types armed with two or three treble hooks. Some skippers have found that plugs designed for surface use, when trolled in the depths, sometimes work even better than those designed specifically for underwater use. This trick has been especially successful in the waters off Sandy Hook, New Jersey. Swimming plugs, like spoons, offer a maximum of built-in action and require far less rod handling than do artificials that lack wobble-plates. It should be noted that plugs occasionally make good use of limber pork-rind strips attached to their tail hooks. More often, rind is used as a sweetener on spoons and jigs.

Lures with extra-long nylon skirts have always loaded fish boxes, particularly when the bass are feeding on any member of the herring family. The time-tested Acetta Jig-It-Eel is a perfect example of the type and, of course, there are numbers of look-alikes and variations available.

Spoons range in size from miniatures on up to the almost gargantuan bunker spoon which is supposed to resemble a struggling menhaden or mossbunker. Usually armed with a large single hook, or two singles rigged ice-tong fashion, the plate-sized offering flops, churns, and probably clangs and clatters in progress. Many are sure that the resulting sound waves, in addition to flash and action, seduce stripers.

Sound also appears to be important to the effectiveness of swimming plugs, and there is good reason to believe that bass are attracted by a sort of aquatic tumult that we do not fully understand and have never adequately duplicated in designing new lures. Certainly those curious maverick baits built around sound-producing chambers alone have never proven frightfully effective.

Whatever tube lures represent, and they are popularly believed to simulate eels, sea worms, or other elongated forage, all are characterized by writhing, sinuous action in the water. Surgical tubing is available in various diameters, lengths, and colors; it is easily cut to shape and rigged with a single hook, or with two hooks positioned line-astern. Every tackle shop on the striper coast offers proven models.

In addition to tubes, other soft plastic baits work well. These include facsimiles of eels—with or without wobble-plates—pseudo squids, baitfish, and seaworms. Note that exact duplication of a given forage species is not enough to guarantee strikes; an artificial must swim enticingly as it is trolled, or it fails.

Knowledge of local resting and feeding areas frequented by striped bass is highly important and often means the difference between success and failure. Unfortunately for a visiting angler, only experience—and years of it—can build such knowledge. If you choose to go deep in an unfamiliar area, better do so with a local guide or charter skipper at your elbow.

Shallow waters would seem to be the least promising of wire-line areas; yet in some cases a shoal ground is mighty productive, even though the tactics adopted there appear to fracture basic rules. These unorthodox methods include a light tackle challenge with line tests ranging between 20 and 30 pounds. Unlike the offshore norm, it is usually necessary under these conditions to stream at least a full 100-yard shot of metal. In a fathom or less of water, most of this will grind along over the bottom, as will the trailing bait or lure.

Oddly enough, it works, because bass often congregate in shoal water, where they are severely spooked by the passage of a boat. Wearing polarized glasses, one can see pods of stripers split to right and left as a craft approaches them. They are frightened and, having been scared away from a chosen feeding location, they take a few minutes to forget the interruption and return. By the time the lure or bait arrives, slithering along 300 feet behind a small boat's transom, these fish have sagged back to their initial point and have apparently lost the memory of panic.

One warm, blue morning, while Indian-guiding a colleague new to the operation, this 300-foot minimum was amply demonstrated. Competitive and as innovative as anyone on the grounds, our companion decided to shorten his wire by at least a third of the suggested length. Thus, he reasoned, his trolled sea worm would reach the pod of fishes well ahead of ours.

After he had caught a considerable number of unflappable summer flounders, while we methodically racked up stripers, the lesson was driven home. It took an hour of abject failure before the man grinned wryly and admitted that "under these conditions you sure need a lot of string!"

In wire-line trolling with artificial lures it is usually wise to spend considerable time removing weeds and other bottom debris that foul hooks. However, it can be a waste of time if you are dragging a shoal with single or double sea worms on a 1/0 or 2/0 hook. Weed guards on hooks are favored by many, but they do not offer an enormous amount of protection.

No matter. In this case the experienced angler is immediately appraised, by tension on the line and by "feel," of whether he has fouled a glob of sea lettuce, grass, or maybe a clam shell. Incidentally, the "clam bite" is an occupational hazard and is always telegraphed by the oscillating motion of the attached shell.

Anyhow, while dragging natural sea worms, soft weeds appear to be no handicap at all. Bass, obviously scenting a delicious worm, burrow right into that moving blob of garbage to inhale the bait. Therefore, to save time in retrieving and de-fouling, wait a bit. Maybe shoal water stripers dote on a mite of salad prior to the main course.

Shallow water work is best pursued over a sand or clay bottom that is relatively free of rubble, but is most profitable where grass or mussel beds, appearing as "black spots" to helmsmen wearing polarized glasses, provide sunken islands of plenty. One often scores well while working the edges of such patches and even while dragging right through the jungle.

Favored tempters in shallow water—although others will certainly be pressed into service as anglers experiment—are a fresh natural sea worm or versions of the ordinary bucktail jig and the nylon "eel." The latter is basically a lead-head with a lengthier dressing of fiber in a variety of colors. While a full-sized, twin-hooked Jig-It-Eel may do well, a lot of shoal water practitioners prefer shorter overall dimensions—say six inches from bull-headed lead snout to the tag-end of dressing—with a single, upriding hook positioned forward. Streamer flies of various types can pay off on wire, and they need not be very sophisticated—just sparse bucktail or slim hackle. Treble-hooked swimming plugs are a bit too clutching for this particular merry-go-round.

At this writing, the International Game Fish Association does not recognize wire line as kosher in the taking of record game fishes. We predict that it will in the future because there is nothing unsportsmanlike about the art of modern wiring. Certainly it does not guarantee success.

10 · Striper on A Fly

SALT WATER FLY FISHING IS RELATIVELY NEW IN OUR angling world; certainly it does not date back to the writings of Dame Juliana Berners—whose very existence has been questioned—or to that amiable ogler of milkmaids, Izaak Walton. It is unlikely that either of these early songbirds ever wet their feet in brine, for Old Man Ocean was then a cruising ground for traders and freebooters. Moreover, the tackle that Juliana and Izaak used was pretty crude. Indeed, split bamboo rods did not enter the lists until approximately 1850, at which time a handful of mavericks were throwing feathers at American striped bass. Those who experimented, like Frank Forester, favored meticulously dressed English salmon flies.

Forester, who was christened Henry William Herbert, was a British remittance man who became America's first well-known outdoor writer. He tangled with bass on a long rod at least a decade prior to his death in 1858. An advocate of the fly rod, Forester wrote ". . . with the sole exception of salmon fishing, this [striped bass fishing] is the finest of the seaboard variations of piscatorial sport . . ."

Certainly there were long-rod pioneers on striper grounds before the turn of the century, but no real popularity surfaced until the late Joseph W. Brooks, Jr. decked his 29-pound, 6-ounce bass at Coos Bay, Oregon, in September, 1948. Joe was tapered down to a 12-pound-test tippet and he used a large white balsa-wood popping bug made to his order by the late Bill Upperman of Atlantic City, New Jersey. Brooks gave us a yellow-painted facsimile of that tempter: It is armed with a 3/0 Z-Nickle hook, then thought to be an advance and now considered far inferior to stainless steel.

A few writers, recording this catch, erroneously stated that the lure was a white streamer. Maybe it does not matter, but Joe, who was the mildest and most courteous of men, was irritated. He grumbled, "Why can't they get it right? Jimmie Christianson was there, guiding us, and our party included Joe Bates, Don Harger, and Chan Brown. It was a white popper, and on that afternoon I hooked another bass at least as big as the first one, maybe bigger."

Prior to Brooks' then sensational trophy, a triumph that was widely publicized and that launched the fly and the popping bug as lures with which to take stripers, there were other names to conjure with—sports-minded individuals building fresh legends on bassing grounds during the mid to late 1920s through the 1930s and right up to the outbreak of Hitler's war. We will neglect a few, yet among the famed innovators were such as the brothers Frank and Harold Gibbs of Rhode Island, Harvey Flint of the same state, Tom Loving of Maryland, Monk Montague in Virginia, Bill and Morrie Upperman of New Jersey, Ollie Rodman of Massachusetts, and former governor of Nevada, Morley Griswold, who pioneered fly casting for stripers.

More recent history documents a massive upwelling of interest from the late 1950s through the present time. Now fly-rodding takes its rightful place among the disciplines favored by striper enthusiasts, and the art annually adds new converts, a host of highly skilled casters building fresh knowledge over the foundations of yesterday. Attribute this enthusiasm in equal parts to improvements in tackle and the inherent challenge of the sport.

When Joe Brooks popularized the game, all equipment was split bamboo. Joe liked a 9-foot rod and a GAF forward-taper line. Indeed some

Henry Lyman, casts from a grassy marsh bank, chancing a tangle if the loose line wraps around the stems below.

classicists of the late 1940s chuckled because he regularly advocated GAF as a sort of all-purpose line for salt water work. At the time, the more sophisticated letter and numeral designations were still in the future tense, urged by such stalwarts as the late Myron Gregory of California.

Lines have been improved and silk, as a basic material, has vanished from the scene. Brooks liked a floating forward-taper and the GAF that matched his 9-foot striper stick would now be called WF-9-F, which indicates Weight-Forward, Number 9, Floating. Joe spoke the language of the mid 1940s and, of course, embraced constructive changes in nomenclature as they came along. He knew that it is essential to ensure a balance between rod and line. Today's manufacturers plot the weight and action factors that will prove most effective and usually print this information on a rod's shaft.

Weapons systems—and that is the right term—have never before approached today's excellence. The old-timers had to work with equipment that now belongs to romantic memory—rods made of various inferior woods or laminations, not to mention impossible metal shafts; single-action reels that were poorly designed by modern standards; lines made of oil-treated silk that in middle age often seemed coated with molasses; no decent synthetic leaders; and a mighty slim assortment of fly types.

Marine fly rod lengths have changed little during the past few decades. On striper grounds 8½ to 9 feet remains about average and there is current emphasis on the short, often detachable extension butt. The major change lies in the building materials. Almost nobody uses split bamboo in the salt, simply because the lovely old split cane is trouble-prone when exposed to the ravages of brine and because the more powerful bamboo rods are heavy and fatiguing to use over any period of time.

Now, and almost certainly within the immediately foreseeable future, synthetics—such as tubular fiberglass, graphite, boron, and calculated mixtures of man-made resins and fibers—rule the angler's roost. These are lighter, stronger, and more efficient than anything produced yesterday. They are quality-controlled, so that each stick in a maker's line is precisely identical to others just removed from the production line. Finally, price has been held to a happy medium.

Two-piece fly rods predominate, although you can buy four- or even six-sectioned models that lend themselves to storage or transportation where space is limited. It is true that the ideal, as in almost any rod for use on site, is one piece. Such a shaft defeats the minor problems which have to do with ferrule design, overall strength, and flawless action from butt to tip top.

Yet we will never see a plethora of these in sporting goods shops. That is because the one-piece fly rod is an abomination to transport, by ground or air, and it hardly lends itself to home storage, particulary when the owner abides in a man-swarmed city. Therefore, practically all of these nice weapons are custom-built.

Fly rods may or may not feature extension butts. Reels should have spools large enough to handle a forward-taper line and 150 to 200 yards of 20- to 30-pound test dacron backing. Floating bugs and streamer flies are the favored lures.

We had a tubular fiberglass model built a number of years ago by Spinmaster. It is a very big stick with a six-inch extension butt, intended to subdue trophy tarpon and calibrated to handle 11- or 12-weight lines. The rod overpowers a majority of striped bass. The thing is not too weepy to rack on a beach buggy, and it is sudden death on junior-grade bass in the wash. One can throw 100 feet with relative ease and, tapered down to a far from ladylike 15-pound-test tippet, winch schoolies ashore in better than jig time.

Aside from a trend toward double-action, smooth, adjustable drags and superior workmanship, reels feature little in the way of drastic evolution. Single-action reels remain the most popular. In its price range one cannot fault the old Pflueger Medalist, which is perfectly capable of subduing trophy stripers. More sophisticated and comparatively expensive marine reels are a joy to use and own, but they are not indispensable on bassing grounds.

There is not a great deal of false casting in salt water, a practice often overdone on inland trout streams where arm-waving serves two purposes: first, to work out a sufficient length of level- or double-taper and, second, to shake the water off a soggy dry fly. In the brine, when you are seeking striped bass and a majority of other marine fishes, a forward-taper line eases your labor. You have about 30 feet of heavy casting head out and ready to go. Another 30 to 60 feet of finer-diameter running line is coiled on the boat's deck, in a waste basket, or looped and held in the left hand. Some showoffs, and we wish we could master the art, hold the loops between their lips.

Anyhow, with forward-taper, one need only initiate a quick pickup, make a strong backcast and follow with a power drive toward the target. Loosely coiled running line is kept manageable by funneling it through a "guide" formed by the thumb and index finger of the left hand—assuming, of course, that the angler is right-handed. Sharpies, tensed for an immediate cast, always have that 30 feet of big taper out beyond the rod's tip to facilitate a quick pickup and throw.

Practice this technique and it soon becomes second nature. Lots of aces go one step further, holding the fly or bug in the left hand while the forward-taper is bellied and the running line is coiled, ready to shoot. With or without double-haul, execution is rapid. Sixty to 70 feet is prime killing range and not at all difficult to reach if the tackle is balanced and the technique reasonably correct. Basic fly casting is rather easily mastered.

There are a number of line types to consider, and some of them are quite specialized. A majority of anglers favor weight-forward-floating because it is easiest to handle and ideal on surface-feeding game. Good-tempered feather merchants will also use sinking-tip-floating (to get down a foot or three), sinking, or fast-sinking versions where needed. Shooting heads are popular for distance throwing and these include lead-core lines to probe the utmost depths. "Heads" are well named: They are separate, relatively short forward sections, usually about 25 to 30 feet in length, with a fine-diameter level-line as backing. Some still use monofilament for backing, although it is inferior to a quality level such as a #3, which keeps fouling and tangling to a minimum.

Line color seems of little importance in striped bass fishing. We prefer white or flourescent shades, simply because these stand out against blue or green backgrounds and are thus easier to control both in casting and retrieve. Backing *is* a necessity and braided dacron, thanks to its lack of stretch, is most efficient. Twenty-pound test ought to suffice on bass, but 30 adds insurance and is our choice. The standard fly line measures 90 to 125 feet. Follow this front strand with as much backing as possible on a given reel and secure it with a spliced loop or a nail knot. A loop is superior if lines are changed often. Despite its good reputation, we have had the nail knot fail under stress and it must be tied very carefully.

Fortunately, the striped bass is rarely exceptionally leader-conscious, so the length may be no more than seven to nine feet from butt to tippet. A lot of successful bass fishermen never taper at all; they simply use a hank of mono of a particular strength and do very well, as long as it turns the lure over at the opportune moment in touchdown. Leader color is always good for a mild argument; the norm, perhaps because it satisfies the human eye, is nearly colorless—light blue, light green, or a shade of tan.

It must be admitted that we have witnessed occasions when school bass would not take a fly or any other tempter when it was presented on too heavy a leader. It is quite possible that rejection was not due to the diameter of the trace or its stiffness, but to the inhibition of the lure action. Fine tippets are limber and so enhance the motion of an armed fooler. One usually employs sectional blood-knotted leaders tapered down to whatever is deemed the essential tippet test, either for ham-handed production or to qualify for IGFA record. In our opinion the one-piece extruded tapered leader is the most efficient, for this guarantees only one questionable, lumpy, little weed-catching connection.

Where bass are the prime targets, tippet strength may be whatever you desire. As a rule of thumb on middleweight to heavyweight stripers, 10-pound test may be a mite daring, while 15 approaches the clout that might be called "unlimited" in marine fly casting. Fifteen is mighty hard to part even under a resilient rod's maximum loading. Note that IGFA rules allow a shock tippet not longer than 12 inches and, where large bass are sought, this can be an advantage. Stripers boast no razor-sharp cutting teeth, but they have a mouth full of sandpaper capable of grinding through a light tippet during any lengthy slug-fest. Wire shockers are unnecessary: 30- to 40-pound mono suffices and is the logical choice.

What are the debits and credits of the discipline? Initially, any long and resilient rod is forgiving: After hookup, a bass is less likely to break off than is one fastened to a strand of similar test complementing a spinning or conventional outfit. There is also greater margin for error. In fact, in exceptionally thin water, such as that encountered when fish are feeding on small bait in a few inches of suds, a streamer fly or buoyant bug succeeds more often than any plug or quick-sinking metal lure.

The undeniable handicaps of the system are threefold. First, presentation of a fly is limited to a relatively short range: 70 to about 100 feet approaches redline. Second, fly or bug size cannot approach that of truly big lures when trophy bass demand them. Third, although stripers are not speed merchants, sometimes they want an offering zipping along at a velocity the fly caster finds hard to match—even with the rod's butt tucked between his legs while he employs a hand-over-hand retrieve.

After the usual clubhouse bragging sessions, most of us make the remarkable discovery that, with or without double-haul, any attempt at a 100-foot touchdown with a big, fluffy, bulky fly or bug induces frustration. A few specialists reach that distance with apparent ease. Most of us cannot, particulary when plagued by the coastal winds. If said wind is in your teeth, a low, hard, power drive is necessary; otherwise the cast balloons and goes nowhere. When gusting from an after quarter, port, or starboard, strange things happen and occasional hooks end up stuck in someone.

It is an error and it is self-defeating to decry the abilities of long-casters, as long as they are not casters first and anglers second. The former, usually refugees from sanitized tournament fields, will often throw 100 feet or better, then pick it all up after 20 feet of retrieve, and throw again. Every cast should be fished out while it covers potentially productive ground. Also, the closer to home a bass strikes, the more securely he will be hooked on a short, taut line. Away out there at the end of a grunt-and-groan cast, your trophy too often has slack in his favor and may well spit the artificial.

The first time we met Lefty Kreh, many years ago, our egos were shattered. At the time we had no knowledge of Lefty's ability and a waggish friend had said that he was a beginner, "so don't make him feel like a chump by throwing a long line."

All went well for a time: we caught a few school stripers at the usual, easy 50- to 60-foot range. Then Kreh stripped *all* the fly line off his reel's spool and coiled it on our boat's deck. This supposed "beginner" then picked up 30 feet of forward-taper and made what appeared to be an ordinary cast. Swiftly, still recounting one of the mad and humorous tales for which he has become famous, the man laid his rod down against a bow seat, stuck both hands in his pockets, and wheeled around to complete his story.

Barry Gibson uses a small boat to cast for bass feeding in one of Maine's coastal rivers.

Suddenly we were saucer-eyed and deflated, because that running line—all of it, plus a few feet of backing—went hissing toward a far horizon. Zap! More than 100 feet, smoothly, effortlessly! It was difficult to refrain from cussing him in several languages.

We hastily note, in passing on to subjects less personally traumatic, that Lefty fishes out his casts on striper grounds and is as accomplished an angler as he is a great showman and teacher of the art. Some experiences, even if tinged with humor in recollection, are not immediately appreciated.

There was, for example, one gale-lashed morning during a New Jersey outdoor writers' convention when a friend got a 3/0 hook stuck right through the lobe of an ear. This episode is related second hand, for we were not on the scene. Having studied a poisonously yellow sunset and checked TV weather predictions the night before, we had loftily forecast high winds and rough water in the following dawn—and therefore spent a pleasant, albeit costly, night playing poker with assorted fellow travelers.

About mid-morning, bleary-eyed and counting our losses, we thought it polite to meet the bedraggled guides, visiting experts, and hopeful writers who had been brave enough to challenge Barnegat Bay in a Force-five fury. They came in fishless, cold, and wet. The friend we mentioned had a Band-Aid on one ear. Bitterly he muttered, "One of your famous salt water authorities tried to take my head off."

The wound was minor and a helpful guide had clipped the protruding barb and backed out the hook's bend with no alarming gush of blood. All hands expressed sympathy while inwardly roaring with laughter—not at the victim, but because the perpetrator was a highly knowledgeable colleague who had, just the day before and in one of the country's most prestigious metropolitan newspapers, printed an alarmist story about clods who fail to exercise caution while casting a fly in a high wind!

Unlike inland specialists, marine feather merchants speak only of flies and bugs, the first usually falling into the general category of streamer and used at various depths, and the second a buoyant popper or slider featuring cork, Styrofoam, balsa-wood, hollow plastic, or—that refugee from fresh water—a tidbit made of tightly packed, trimmed-to-shape deer hair. For the tempting of striped bass, these surface offerings range in size from miniatures like Cap Colvin's old Ca-Boom-Boom up to the largest floaters that can be cast to a reasonably distant mark. This usually means a type armed with a 1/0 to 3/0 hook, graced by sparse dressing of hair or feathers aft. Overall length is anywhere from three to about five inches, and the bug's face is either cupped, cut to a diagonal slant up front, or bullet-nosed. The object is to create either commotion or the switching progress of a disoriented bait fish struggling in surface film.

The aforementioned Ca-Boom-Boom is simply a scaled-down bug, easy to throw and, because of its slim silhouette and buoyancy, particularly deadly

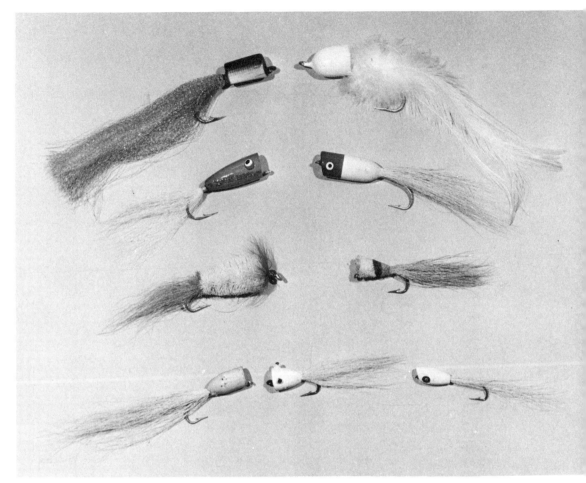

Floating bugs stir up commotion and often hook heavy bass. Those pictured here, with the exception of the slider (top right) are popping types.

when schoolies are foraging in thin water, often right up against the surf's shingle. Granted, we have never tied into a genuine trophy with this junior-grade lovely, but the job has been done by many others.

The nature of streamer fly pattern on marine grounds remains arguable and even the definition of the word "pattern" itself differs from that accepted by purists on inland trout and salmon streams. There are a few "striper patterns," such as the famed Gibbs designs, the Blondes that Joe Brooks popularized, Lefty's Deceiver, and Russell Chatham's Black Phantom, among others. But are they true patterns? We hold most to be types, rarely approaching the nearly rigid blueprint of the inland fly.

The Gibbs and a few others are kosher, although they are seldom used nowadays. Brooks' Blondes come in a wide variety of colors, owing their

Streamer fly "pattern" is arguable, but types or series are used in a number of sizes and dressings.

effectiveness primarily to a fore-and-aft dressing calculated to ensure maximum length without bulk. Lefty's Deceiver, an excellent type, goes the same route, since there are several recommended dressings and the only thing that appears remotely constant is a touch of mylar to add glitter. Some folk add strip lead to a hook's shank prior to dressing. Many employ additional tinsel, whether or not the originator called for this.

It is possible that true pattern will evolve on striper grounds. Do we need it? At this moment one can succeed with a simple bucktail or feather offering in white, yellow, green and white, or black. Every hue has its own champions, and classic anglers are forever insisting upon flawless construction, even though this may not afford an edge and even though spoil-sports insist that sea-oriented bassers who swear by exact replicas of proven flies—of which there are almost none—are engaged in wishful thinking.

Striped bass are somewhat catholic in their tastes. Phil Schwind, a Cape Cod charter skipper and one-time commercial rod-and-liner, likes bushy green-and-white bucktail creations roughly lashed to 6/0 hooks, and he has always caught a lot of bass. Similarly, throngs of new and highly competent masters of the fly rod each in turn boasts a "pattern" that he has personally developed and holds to be ideal. All of them catch fish, but we must define them as types, not exact facsimiles of universally accepted dressings such as those collector's items tied by crotchety little Theodore Gordon on the banks of the Neversink.

Please do not shoot from the hip! We are fully aware of the fact that Gordon subtly changed the basic hues of his dressing according to the seasons and his needs, but not by much. Once it was developed, he stuck to his pattern and his admitted variations digressed only by a slight nuance of wing or hackle color. The Quill Gordon to this day is still clearly a Quill Gordon.

Predictably there is a paucity of interest in salt water versions of the nymph and dry fly, or indeed in any copies of ephemeridae, which in the larval or flying stage are as rare in the brine as bluefish with false teeth. It may be argued that shrimp and crab simulations are closest to nymphs, but of course both are crustaceans.

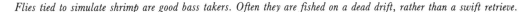

Flies tied to simulate shrimp are good bass takers. Often they are fished on a dead drift, rather than a swift retrieve.

Since bass often feed on shrimp, imitations are fairly plentiful and frequently succeed. Most of them have a somewhat humpbacked configuration and are therefore best presented on a dead drift. However, recent years have seen greater experimentation with straight and streamlined facsimiles which lend themselves to a slow retrieve close to the surface or at any depth down to eelgrass country. Both versions should be included in a well-stocked tackle box.

As far as small and scuttling crabs are concerned, we have not detected a frantic rush to dress look-alikes such as we have seen on the tropical flats where sportsmen seek permit and bonefish. Seaworms make snacks for stripers, so tyers often build pseudo-squirmers with deep red or almost maroon hair tied sparsely. The fly is particularly effective when "Mayworms," the immature stage of the sea worms' life cycle, are free-swimming in coastal waters. Usually this artificial takes schoolies, but big bass have been known to muscle in on the act.

When this book first saw publication in 1954, we damned with faint praise any activated fluorescent lure. To a certain extent that assessment has been modified, for, regularly enough to excite interest, these neon-like tempters are highly successful. Blaze orange has fared best for us, with hot pink a close runner-up, both appearing to be most effective on a cloudy or fog-shrouded day. It is quite possible that a bass mistakes this glowing streamer or bug for a small and delectable squid.

Much attention has been lavished on producing imitation sand eels. Indeed, we once created a type which, because it employed a variety of different colors in dressing, was first named "the snake series." We gave it length by using a section of hollow mylar piping extended well aft of the hook's bend. True pattern ends right there, for the piping can be either silver or gold and the wings are either hair or saddle hackle tied sparsely. The finished artificial is easy to cast, boasts a proper silhouette, and certainly catches the odd bass. The "snake" is now used on just about every coast and has its fair share of names, such as "Tomahawk," "Candlefish," and plain "Sand Eel" for those lacking in imagination. All are slightly fragile, since mylar piping frays rapidly in use.

Few inventors of fly patterns or types are named in this book, simply because it is difficult to pinpoint the origin of any widely accepted artificial. Patents are not applied for, and honest anglers often think that they have made a breakthrough when they have only produced a variation or popularized an early approach to perfection. There is an old soldier's wry explanation for defeat in battle after careful planning, and it fits here: "Success has many fathers, but failure is always an orphan."

All fly tyers embrace certain rules of thumb, which are occasionally and successfully flouted. Thanks to the necessity to cast well and reasonably far, and for the fly to swim enticingly, sparse dressing often is favored. It has even been said that bushy flies are made to catch fishermen, not fish; but there are happy days when a fluffy type that breathes in the water triumphs. Carbon steel hooks are strong and sharp, but stainless steel has swiftly supplanted the rust-prone article.

Overall size and the effort to "match the hatch" on site are important. It has been said to the point of cliché that one should always favor big baits for big fish. That is true most of the time, but striped bass are selective and the largest lineside in the sea may prove to be a patsy for a miniature tidbit. Knowing this, modern fly casters never discount the effectiveness of a tiny lure.

Short-shanked hooks often suffice with streamer flies, since bass tend to inhale them, but bend and barb should extend beyond the bug's body, although not beyond the limber tail dressing. The reason is that a striper attempting to eat a lure that is progressing through surface film creates a considerable bow wave in front of itself, which can knock the offering right out of its mouth. You will miss some furious strikes in any event, but a long-shanked bug hook saves a great many of them. When a bass makes no contact at all it is likely to be excited and intent on coming back. Try to avoid a quick reflex "set" as the white water spouts. Feel unmistakable pressure before hitting the beast and you will be in solid. This is never so necessary with a submerged streamer, because the quarry seems to zero in accurately and swiftly.

Trolling a big streamer pattern can be mighty effective, although it is not accepted as fly casting. The benefits include a choice of lines and lure sizes. For some reason, perhaps because the average feather merchant is something of a purist where striped bass are concerned, the practice is not employed as regularly as it is on some offshore species, such as dolphin.

A somewhat modified fly rod is commonly used in light trolling, where the lures may be small wobbling spoons, sub-surface swimming plugs, or spinner-and-worm combinations. In this case, gung-ho folk may replace their snake guides with good quality rings to ensure an easier passage of wire as well as monofilament. The resulting rod, graced by a balanced line, may still be used to cast flies, but it will be unwieldy and heavy for that office.

It is natural to think of fly casting as a daylight operation, yet it can be quite as effective during the hours of darkness, especially when the bass are chasing small bait, such as sand eels, right into the suds. Probably the largest striper ever taken on a fly in the surf fell to H. K. "Kib" Bramhall of Vineyard Haven, Massachusetts, on October 16, 1981. Using a four-inch-long, predominantly yellow Lefty's Deceiver armed with a 1/0 stainless steel hook, Kib played and beached a 42-pound, 14-ounce lineside. The hour of hookup was 5:15 A.M. prior to first light, and Bramhall's tackle was far from heavy—a 3.8-ounce, 8½-foot graphite rod and a small, inexpensive single-action reel. The place was Chappaquiddick, at the east end of Martha's Vineyard.

The major concern in nighttime surf casting with a fly rod is to avoid muscling into a picket line of anglers using much heavier gear, thereby inviting horrific tangles and straining more tempers than tackle. Courtesy is just as important under a noonday sun. Mannerly people who are jockeying big spinning and conventional outfits never crowd the lone fly caster.

Naturally, it can be a journey into frustration to throw flies into a big surf where control is almost impossible. Your results will be more spectacular if you work from a boat and cover known striper hidey-holes—the reasonably quiet points, rips, rock piles, weed and shell beds that tend to hold concentrations of feeding fish. The fly rod is well chosen in a sheltered bay, estuary, or brackish river system, and frequenters of coastal sod banks find the bass obliging.

Suppose now that you have hooked a good fish and he is running doggedly. The long wand will wear him down fairly quickly, and landing the trophy becomes the final challenge. Shorebound anglers whose lines aren't tapered down to fine tippets can always ride the catch to safety on a handy ground swell after said trophy has become thoroughly exhausted. Gaffs remain in common use, but a wide-mouthed landing net is far better, except in pounding surf, and this tool is favored by a majority of fly casters.

It would be sorry propaganda to declare that fly casting solves all the problems in striped bass fishing; yet this art provides classic sport, delicacy in the presentation of featherweight lures, and, under optimum conditions, fish galore.

11 · Ancillary Equipment

THEORETICALLY, AN ANGLER IS FULLY ARMED WHEN he sallies forth with rod, reel, line, and lure. Actually, the confirmed basser covets a great deal more in the way of supporting weapons, clothing, and basic tools geared to the specialized game plans of boat or beach. Some enthusiasts desire a private plane to spot fish that are loafing on offshore bars, a sophisticated boat, or a four-wheel-drive beach buggy. All contribute rich frosting to an already delicious piece of cake, and each is uniquely practical in its own sphere of operation. However, other and far less expensive items of ancillary equipment are truly essential to the comfort and working efficiency of a striped bass fisherman.

Before examining the basics, consider the aforementioned trio of prime movers—noting with a measure of wry satisfaction that one can conquer a trophy lineside without such aids. Obviously, a well-found boat is most important of all, since it is a magic carpet for the complete angler who practices several rod-and-line disciplines, from sheltered waters to high surf to offshore banquet tables. (See Chapter 8 for a discussion of modern hull design and sea-going techniques.)

Light airplanes that provide rapid transportation to coastal air strips, which often are located a couple of miles away from fishing grounds, are cursed by inadequate baggage space and are regularly grounded by the inclement weather that is so likely to coincide with a striper blitz. It is indeed true that from a low altitude one can locate concentrations of fish and fishermen on a potential killing ground. However, today's regulations increasingly prohibit beach landings by aircraft, so one must transfer from the plane to a ground vehicle after any reconnaissance mission. It is most practical to charter a short spotting flight out of a strip close to the angling scene. Your airplane driver probably will be a striper fisherman himself and he will know what to look for.

Beach buggies, briefly defined, are all-terrain motor vehicles designed to carry anglers and their duffel to and from remote fishing areas. There are two basic types, so the mechanized sportsman must choose one that serves his specific needs. A surprising number of affluent regulars blithely invest in *two* machines, a somewhat expensive solution and one requiring a brace of drivers.

First, and undoubtedly more often seen on today's beaches, is what is commonly described as a "chase car." We coined that term some years ago and it has become generic for any of the small, tough vehicles widely employed as tackle and personnel carriers. Almost all are four-wheel-drive models, sophisticated descendants of America's military Jeep. They are extraordinarily nimble, but bereft of the interior space needed to install creature comforts. We nicknamed them chase cars simply because they resemble light cavalry mounts for surf fishing corsairs, ideal in the pursuit of bass distributed along an expanse of beach.

Ardent mechanized anglers sometimes hit the beach with one big live-in beach buggy and a smaller "chase car," plus a surf boat. Most of the vehicles feature four-wheel drive.

Second of the currently most popular types is a big live-in vehicle which may be a coach camper or a walk-in truck. Large, heavy, but surprisingly functional when possessed of sufficient power, four-wheel drive, and proper flotation tires, these battleships of the dunes progress slowly, but rarely bog down. Often, now that wives and gaggles of suntanned children have become equal partners on the fishing beaches, these machines are literally homes away from home. They boast the clean beds and white sheets soldiers are supposed to dream about, stainless steel galleys and running water, refrigerating units, self-contained toilet facilities, separate lighting, central heating where necessary, even TV sets. This is hardly a machine designed to "rough it" out in the open, but maybe it conserves bass by providing plush comfort when a fish-filled surf is storm-lashed and cold.

Compromise choices are represented by carry-all types and pick-up trucks with small camper units mounted aft. These cannot match the mountain-goat agility of the Jeep styles, nor are they roomy enough to accommodate many creature comforts. However, the machines move well on soft tracks and they are easily converted to family use between fishing expeditions.

A great many sand dune jockeys are craftsmen who enjoy working with one another. Therefore master mechanics, metal workers, plumbers, and electricians swap personal talents. Most are members of one of the coastal beach buggy associations, tightly knit organizations in which every card-carrying man and woman seems dedicated to Kipling's poetic dictum, "The strength of the pack is the wolf, and the strength of the wolf is the pack." The vehicles owned by club members are rigged to work.

The first aim for beach-buggy owners is flawless performance on the beach *and* on the highways linking their favored grounds. Obviously, the tires must have adequate road treads, yet be of ample size to support weight in soft going. Even four-wheel drive, now universally preferred, will labor unless tire pressures are dropped from what they are for paved road. The correct level of deflation depends on the consistency of the sand encountered, so every driver carries—and may be required to carry in order to obtain an off-road permit—a pressure gauge, a suitable jack, and a hardwood plank on which to base the jack, a tow-chain, and a shovel. A majority of pilots install air compressors on their engine mounts.

Often there is a cargo box bolted to a small vehicle's roof, together with a boat rack. However, light 12- to 14-foot planing skiffs are now less popular than larger motor boats, which must be trailered. Since manhandling is no longer feasible, a perfectionist will bolt a power-driven winch to the center of his car's bumper, plus a padded ram located well to the left. Big, open-console craft are pushed into the suds, then winched high and dry after each full-throttle landing.

Whether you are using a chase car or a home on wheels, there must be adequate duffel space for items of tackle, a tool box, a spare tire, and some sort of a container in which to transport fish. For highway travel, long rods

Famed angler and lure-maker Stan Gibbs with a battery of rods racked vertically on the front bumper of a "chase car."

are racked on horizontally aligned, spring-loaded clips. On the beach, ready-to-use sticks go into heavy, vertical aluminum or hard plastic pipes welded or bolted to the front or rear bumpers. Since each surfman wants to tote a considerable amount of tackle, he will plan to utilize every square inch of available duffel space.

Beach driving is an art which can only be learned by experience. There is no close parallel, although some liken it to plowing through a foot of snow. The difference between snow and soft sand is that the latter does not guarantee a foundation. When you start to "spin in," you go down like a demented elevator, and gunning the motor only aggravates the difficulty. Spinning in is immediately followed by digging out, an operation that means jacking, filling, and shoring up with driftwood planks.

In really soft going, one must "track" like a tank, accelerate cautiously, keep well above the treacherous low tide line, and forget the brakes. Never, a thousand times never, park overnight where a high course tide can inundate your machine. Once, on Cape Cod, we awoke in the middle of the night to find that an unexpected hurricane wind had driven a flood much higher than we had anticipated. Almost two feet of angry water was swirling around the wheels of our machine as it settled deeper and deeper in the shifting sand.

Fortunately that was the top of that gale-driven tide and we suffered little more than momentary panic, sand-clogged brake drums, and sore backs from digging out the next morning.

Over-sand vehicles have been evolving ever since a few adventurous pioneers stuck balloon tires on Model-A Fords, well before World War II. However, interest remained academic until GI Joe came marching home in 1945 and 1946. At that time the Model-A, now a collector's item, swiftly gained favor as a seaside mount. Other light two-wheel drive automobiles were pressed into service and, within a few years, there was a trend toward walk-in trucks rehabilitated after their weary years on suburban milk routes. The first of the four-wheel drives were war surplus Jeeps, command cars, and retired ambulances. Like all military wheeled hardware, these relics were difficult to maintain because the parts differed from those built into domestic models. Even so small a thing as a set of spark plugs had to be scrounged from some friend who worked in an Army motor park.

A few two-wheel-drive vehicles still ply American beaches, but most of the highway queens lack sufficient ground clearance and mechanical guts to

Immediately after World War II beach buggies were vintage Fords and other light highway machines. All were rigged for cruising the dunes.

long survive labor beyond the call of civilian duty. Moreover, increasing numbers of town, state, and federal beach management authorities demand four-wheel drive wherever off-highway machines are allowed to operate. Because of restrictive regulations—many of which mechanized anglers feel to be arbitrary, politically inspired, and totally unfair—the future of the classic beach buggy is uncertain.

Although it has been stated, with some degree of accuracy, that a bass fisherman is less concerned with comfort than good fishing, no striper enthusiast likes to be wet and cold. Ragged cotton trousers may comprise the uniform on a sunny afternoon in high summer, but there are more occasions when it is necessary to dress like a sub-arctic caribou hunter. Spring and fall on either coast calls for long-handled underwear and plenty of woolens topped by foul-weather gear. Indeed abnormally low summer temperatures and chilly nights dictate at least the instant availability of warm clothing through-out bassing season. An extra shirt or a windbreaker can make the difference between a miserable trip and a highly pleasant one.

Goose-down padded garments, together with those stuffed with other organic or synthetic fiber insulation, are extremely lightweight and warm. They "breathe," thereby preventing the accumulation of moisture from per-spiration; their only handicap is their utter lack of efficiency when they are soaked by a steady downpour or by dashing spray or wave action on a comber-lashed beach. Padded clothing drenched down is clammy and cold and it does not retain warmth when wet, as does time-honored wool. Still, when it is fluffy and reasonably dry, nothing is quite so comforting as the feather-padded article.

Warm feet, warm body, it is said. Certainly footwear should be selected to serve a specific purpose. Today's marketplace offers a wide selection of boots, waders, and boat shoes. Rope soles are hard to beat on the slippery deck of a bounding bass boat, and these may be had with leather or canvas uppers. Rubber soles, cut to a squeegee design, also grip well on slick wet decks. The half-boot featuring a grip sole is an ideal choice; it is both comfortable and efficient in defeating slop before it streams out of scuppers. Never go aboard wearing hobnails or other metal cleats, a practice that enfuriates otherwise gentle sea dogs. Hip-length rubber boots are not very practical out beyond harbor bounds, and waders should be left ashore: Although they turn spray and afford a measure of warmth, the things are clumsy in cockpit or cabin and they introduce a definite element of danger if, Lord forbid, one happens to topple overboard.

Hip boots often get the nod for river, canal, or sod bank fishing, but waders are favored by surf casters who challenge the big breakers. For greatest comfort these should be the chest-high models, roomy enough to ensure ease in walking and bending from the waist. It is only good sense to order about one size larger than that considered correct in dry land footwear, if only to provide space for an extra pair of woolen socks and maybe a felt innersole. Pay attention to inseam leg length: One too long for your frame will create sagging drapes and discomfort, while one too short will bind and therefore hamper walking or clambering over weedy rock piles. The very best of these garments are custom-made; they are comparatively expensive—and worth every dime of extra cost.

In purchasing waders, understand that a compromise is involved. Ideally, this garment should be tough, snag-proof, and lightweight—a triumvirate of virtues often difficult to combine. Stout rubber or nicely fabricated, reasonably heavy synthetic-faced articles may be the closest to all-purpose. Fabric-faced rubber is supremely comfortable, but we have found these to be collectors of gritty sand particles that induce swift abrasion. Ultra-light rubber and various featherweight synthetic materials cannot survive very long where hard labor is the order of the day. They are practical choices when a traveling angler must keep his baggage weight to an absolute minimum. It is false economy to buy flimsy, bargain waders.

Most over-the-counter waders feature boot foot design, are tough and ordinarily functional. Generally, some grip is assured by molded-in rubber cleats which are excellent on a sand beach, but hardly adequate on a rock pile. There, metal studs are essential and patent types may be had at a low cost. Innovative fishermen rig substitutes, such as golf studs or even tin caps salvaged from beer bottles. The last-named rust at flank speed and are generally too flimsy for more than a couple of rounds with barnacled boulders.

One solution, and a good one, is to purchase and wear sandals manufactured for this use alone. They are easy to un-strap so that you will not scar the hardwood floors of seaside friends who offer you a pleasant sanctuary and hot coffee during a break in combat. Strap-on ice creepers, commonly used by inland ice fishermen, will also provide acceptable traction. We cannot recommend the inland trout fisherman's felt soles, since they add no benefit on sand, clay, or mud, and are worthless when an angler tries to negotiate slimy, weed-draped boulders.

Finally there are stocking-foot waders, which are admittedly light and comfortable, although they require specialized boots or, a poor substitute, ankle-high tennis shoes. This type may frustrate marine fishermen when sand grains or pebbles work their way down into each shoe, automatically leading to chafing or, worse, leaks. No substitute exists for the job-rated article. However, surf casters have long worked a dodge with hip boots and foul-weather pants. Boots are secured at the belt line, after which oilskins are drawn over them. Pants legs are then lashed tightly at each ankle, thus preventing any surge of icy brine from coursing up one's shanks and spilling into personal property best kept warm and dry. The trick is a good one to remember, but it is strictly an emergency measure that never entirely ensures against a chill flood.

One boot style is worth avoiding, and that is the type prettily funneled down to tight fit at the ankles. Probably intended to keep socks from "creeping" and bunching up, the design stubbornly resists removal after a wetting.

A fisherman can use a snugged-up waist belt to support his waders, but stout suspenders are better. These are manufactured especially for such use, althouth the tough, inexpensive braces sold as policemen's or firemen's models cannot be improved upon.

Wherever one fishes in the sea, from shore or boat, foul-weather tops and bottoms are indispensable. However, do not be led astray while shopping by cosmetic imitations of the real thing: Extremely lightweight and poorly designed suits, even though exquisitely colored to delight maiden ladies of both sexes, offer neither genuine comfort nor protection. On big, bursting striper grounds insist on tough and truly waterproof foul-weather gear, roomy enough to be comfortable when worn over inner clothing. Color does not matter, although bright yellow or the even more visible fluorescent orange are practical in the unlikely event that one yearns to be spotted by Coast Guard rescue personnel after losing a battle with the Law of General Cussedness.

Thanks to economic moon phases that have induced rising tides of inflation, superior foul-weather gear no longer sells for few dollars. Stocks of surplus ex-Navy tops and bottoms have been depleted, so the only existing source of job-rated and fairly inexpensive garments may be a ship's chandler who sells to hard-bitten commercial fishermen. These suits are rugged and utilitarian, albeit a mite heavy in weight for the average rod-and-reel angler, and lacking the specialized niceties developed by perfectionists catering to the sporting trade.

Ideally, foul-weather gear will shed water better than a duck's back. The material used may be fabric over rubber, although at the moment an inner close weave of non-clinging nylon topped with flexible polyurethane draws the greatest angler applause. There must be a parka hood equipped with a tie-down draw-string, either non-stretch or elasticized. Non-corrosive fastenings are essential and may be either zippers or snaps, or a combination of the two. We do not scorn zippers per se, but too many of them tend to go sticky, crotchety, and bind-prone after a season or two of battling the brine.

Tops, thus secured from neck to waist, are well chosen for offshore work if they can be opened to allow blessed ventilation in bluebird weather. "Waterproof" is variously defined: Zippers and snaps surely discourage the intrusion of spray and mild precipitation, but they will not keep gale-driven rain at bay, and they will fail a wading surf caster.

On *that* merry-go-round, a pull-over top with no frontal opening other than at the neck is far more practical. By the same token, place no zealous trust in elastic at the wrists and waist, for they are bound to flex and allow a sledge hammer wave to swarm in. Draw-strings are more efficient at these points, even if snugged down until they approach discomfort. Keep the wristlet cords as short as possible, else a trailing strand may foul a reel's spool.

Waders eliminate the need for foul-weather pants, but a draw-string at

Waders and long-beaked caps are standard uniform for surf casters. Left to right: Spider Andresen, Rip Cunningham, Henry Lyman, and Barry Gibson. All but Cunningham, who is wearing the usual foul-weather top, tote striped bass. Rip tweaked out a pair of bluefish.

the skirt of a waterproof top is not enough to prevent wetting. Add a leather waist belt or, if you can lay hands on one, an ex-Army infantry web belt that can be adjusted to any size, is fitted with brass grommets on which to secure various items of equipment, and can be cinched up tight enough to spoil the fun of angry seas. Wadered and belted amidships, an eager striper hunter cannot walk on water, but he sure can venture almost neck-deep before suffering any invasion by the cold and briny.

A minor number of athletic folk on both coasts are experimenting with wet suits made for skin divers. These garments are efficient, yet employed by other than competent lads and lasses who can swim nearly as well as the stripers they seek, wet suits may tempt excursions into dangerously current-swept, rock-studded waters. Our records indicate that this "uniform" for surf casting was initially accepted by the anglers of Long Island, New York, and was almost simultaneously adopted by Californians in the San Francisco area. Wet suits can become unbearably hot when the wearer is not at least partially submerged.

Hats remain in style on various sea fronts. We've always preferred the long-beaked swordfisherman's model, yet can offer no argument against the currently popular short-visored baseball cap, whether or not adorned with anchors, braids, and colorful club insignia. The style is practical and one must admit that it is not so easily displaced by wind as the vintage choice. Berets or watch-caps, while lacking any eye-shielding visor, will cling to one's cold or balding pate in a half gale. Unimpressed by the sartorial splendor of friends who live in Texas, we figure a ten-gallon cowboy hat out of the OK Corral on a turbulent striper coast. Of course there is one undeniably good word to be said of all wide-brimmed headpieces: They protect against the broiling sunlight.

Sunglasses cannot be ignored on brilliant beaches or offshore grounds. A variety of types and colors are readily available and they range from the inexpensive to finely ground prescription models. Anglers favor polarized lenses, since they cut surface glare and permit a wearer to "see through the water," in addition to filtering out potentially dangerous infrared and ultraviolet rays. Invariably a dark shade of green, gray, or tan proves most efficient—and the key word is "dark." If one can clearly see a colleague's eyes through his shades, then the lenses admit too much light and are almost worthless for comfort and practical use on a bright seacoast.

Gloves, most often in evidence offshore where big game fishes are wrestled to gaff, are not considered indispensable on a striper coast. However, we have found them comfortable during early spring and late fall sport when temperatures are crispy. Gloves pose no major handicaps when spinning tackle is employed, but must be charged with impeding sensitive control of a revolving-spool reel. In any event, during an abnormal deep-freeze period on a bassing ground, we strongly suggest repairing to warm barracks, fitting the hand around a glass of something tinkley in front of a blazing driftwood log in a fireplace. For kicks, read this book. As crusty military instructors have been growling down through the misty centuries, do as we say—not as we do!

Striper buffs who own spacious beach buggies or sophisticated boats are blessed with adequate duffel space to tote a ton of tackle and equipment. No such load-carrying capacity is enjoyed by those who must depend on a shank's mare. Shorebound stalkers of bass prune to a minimum: Still, depending on time, tactics, and strategy, a few indispensable tools accompany every zealous seeker of game fishes.

A suitable tackle box, unless one plans to meander sea miles down-beach, is not burdensome. In it there will be the usual assortment of favored lures, hooks, sinkers, leaders, and bottom rigs. In our salad days we always referred to this as a ditty box, and the name seems peculiarly apt when such maybe-yes and maybe-no aids to comfort are added, like sunscreen lotion, insect repellent, Band-Aids, and a small packet of aspirin tablets.

No respectable ditty box would be completely stuffed without a phial of bright red fingernail polish to tint lethargic plugs and squids. We go so far as to carry little bottles of red, blue, white and yellow lacquer for touch-up work. This is also the place for extra reel spools and, perhaps, a second reel. Ferrule cement, a heavy cutting pliers, a small screwdriver, a fine-cut file and a carborundum stone are necessities. So is a valve-spout can of light machine oil and a tube of gear grease. If you do not carry a pocket or sheath knife on your person, tuck one into the box, keeping it well-oiled to defeat rust.

The box itself should be of modern design, light in weight, of rugged construction, and featuring compartmented, swing-out trays. Ascertain that the lid or cover clamps down snugly and that it is fitted with a stout latch. A padlock will not prevent thievery, but will guard against an occasional frustrating spill in transit.

A tough, lightweight tackle box is essential. So is this selection of tools, rigging, and lures, to be tucked into each "ditty box."

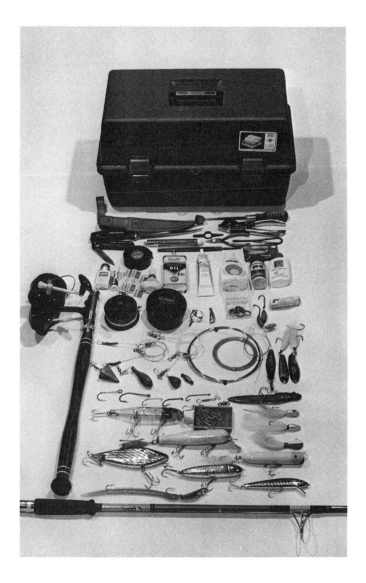

Ancient beachcombers often dispensed with tackle or ditty boxes, and the container they habitually used may be a winner to this day. It is a 16-quart pail, originally a wooden butter tub, which may now exude a patina of romance, yet is no more efficient than a galvanized or hard plastic bucket. The arrangement is still hard to beat. Bait, with a small bedding of moist seaweed, goes into the bottom. Rigs with hooks and sinkers attached, plus metal squids and plugs are suspended inside, dangling from the pail's rim, so loss is held to a minimum. Voila! You're a happy warrior, traveling light.

Today's sanitized surfer travels light too, by attaching ancillary gear to his waist belt or carrying it in a shoulder bag. Within easy reach are sheathed cutting or combined cutting and needle-nosed pliers, a well-honed knife, a stringer to drag the bass he surely will catch, and a compartmented container designed to accommodate a half-dozen lures or bottom rigs. Where it is felt necessary, a short-handled gaff will be there, secured with spirally coiled telephone cord. Bait, in most cases, will be carried separately.

Any or all of these precious essentials may be tucked into a shoulder bag, which may be a blessing or a ho-hum bit of excess baggage. While the thing has a tendency to flop around and get in the way while casting, it can be shrugged off in seconds and temporarily deposited on the beach above a high tide line.

A short club made of hardwood, sometimes loaded, is best strung on a loop of elasticized cord and slung around one's neck to ride comfortably between the shoulder blades until needed. Outlawed in many areas—and it *ought* to be outlawed—is the murderous little blackjack. To the uninitiated, this midget slugger seems beautifully designed to belt a bass into submission. That is sorry theory, because the lead-loaded sap is treacherously limber. After it slams home, the vindictive thing recoils and does its best to smash your knuckles.

A great many striper fishermen feel underprivileged unless they possess certain luxuries which aid in the rapid depletion of bass stock or, at least, make easier the lot of the angler. These items include sand spikes and rod sockets. The former can be a necessity and those marketed by several firms fill the bill. You can make your own by shaping a length of angle iron or galvanized metal to a point, then adding a cup and tool clip to hold the rod in position. We have seen enterprising fishermen fashion a "spike" from a shovel and a stout elastic band. The virtue of a long-bladed spike, or a wide-bladed shovel, is that it will resist the lunge of a bass that hooks itself and is tugging against a drag that is too tightly set up. Lightly anchored sand spikes often permit stripers to decorate themselves with trailing rods, reels, and hooks.

Belt-positioned rod sockets can be mighty helpful in boat or jetty fishing where a short butt is employed, but they are unnecessary in the high surf. Years ago every surf caster thought it necessary to wear an apron bib and cup, or a shaped leather socket, theoretically to take the strain off arms and shoulders, just as an offshore fighting harness does. The idea sounds feasible, but a majority of today's regulars simply tuck a long rod's butt between their legs. The reel is then ideally positioned to play a fish in comfort.

Nobody needs a flying gaff in striped bass fishing, but it makes sense to select various sizes of gaps and handle lengths for specialized use. Short-handled picks are fine in the surf, although sand beach regulars seldom bother with them. When it is possible to ride a fish ashore on a helpful ground swell, one can always grab a stout leader and haul it out of the tinkling wash or swing a club. However, folk teetering on sea-buffeted rock piles or wading deep to throw lures from a promising sand bar make use of this tool, usually capping the point with an attached sponge-rubber ball or other protective sheath to ensure against accidentally sticking it into tender portions of human anatomy. Snap-lock folding gaffs have been manufactured by several firms, yet none seems to have cornered the market.

Points are not really points unless they are needle-sharp. Hone your weapons at home base and touch them up regularly on site. Dull points have lost as many bass as tight reel drags: They merely glance off overlapping scales. Thanks to varying gap sizes and handle lengths, no single gaff is all-

The prime tools at coup de grace *time: a wide-mouthed landing net, gaffs with adequate handle length, and a club to dispatch fish kept for gourmet meals.*

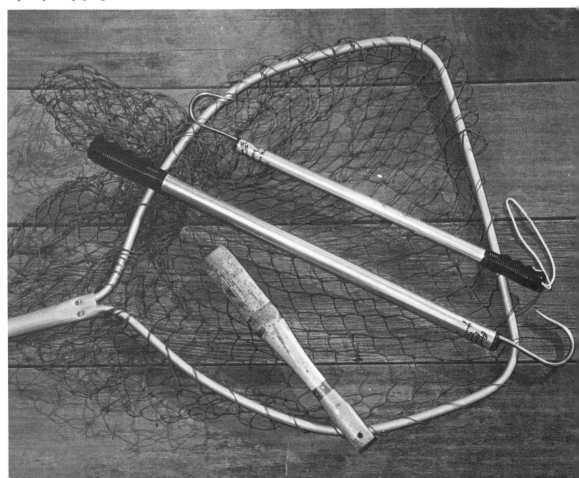

purpose. One seldom needs a king-sized snatcher, for a three- to three-and-one-half-inch spread will stick any average or record lineside. The handle length depends on one factor only: It must be long enough to reach the quarry from a boat's deck or from some precarious perch on the end of a jetty or a rock pile. We would not be without three different configurations: one very short pick featuring standard gap, another very similar hook with a 36-inch-long fiberglass butt section, and a third of similar length, yet armed with a 14/0 extra-strength Martu hook with the barb ground off. This last midget is a pleasant tool to use on schoolies. Our gaff handles are painted white, each bearing a wind or two of fluorescent orange tape. White is easiest to locate at night, and activated orange glows like a neon tube by day, at dawn, or at dusk.

Bassers who operate with fly rods or the more delicate of spinning outfits find wide-mouthed landing nets best of all, particularly when they are dipped from a boat's deck or a sod bank. An increasing number of shallow water trollers also find a net most practical, and it is surely a logical choice when stripers are to be released after capture. That is the scoop, no pun intended—

Ready-made leaders and typical bait hooks. Top left: the fishfinder rig with, first, a bank sinker to hold on rocky ground, and second, a pyramid weight that anchors better in sand or mud.

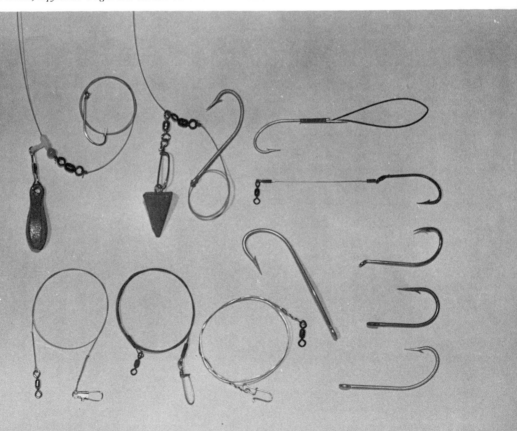

a good rule occasionally broken. Kib Bramhall, whose 42-pound, 14-ounce striper was caught on a fly rod and a yellow Lefty's Deceiver, rode his trophy ashore on a ground swell in pre-dawn darkness. No light, no gaff, no net!

Lights are controversial on every nighttime striper ground. While bass will feed happily under the regular, rotating beam of a coastal lighthouse, they often resent a sudden glare of automobile headlamps or on-again, off-again flashlights. That is why mannerly beach buggy jockeys often switch off their lights, even though this may fracture sand driving regulations, when they pass working surfmen in the suds. Regulars seldom show more than a tiny mote of light while taking the hooks out of a fish, not only because they desire to keep said fish a secret from other anglers, but because they are convinced that undue brilliance will ruin the sport. Hardy types favor tiny two-celled pen lights that can be clipped into a shirt pocket under a foul-weather top when not in use, or a battery-powered miner's headlamp, invariably slung around the neck. Boatmen are just as itchy about excessive incandescence on a midnight sea, to the point of threatening light-happy neighbors with fates worse than a lifetime catching nothing but skates.

These are tools that most surfmen employ. However, the bib-type, rod-holding socket is no longer in great favor.

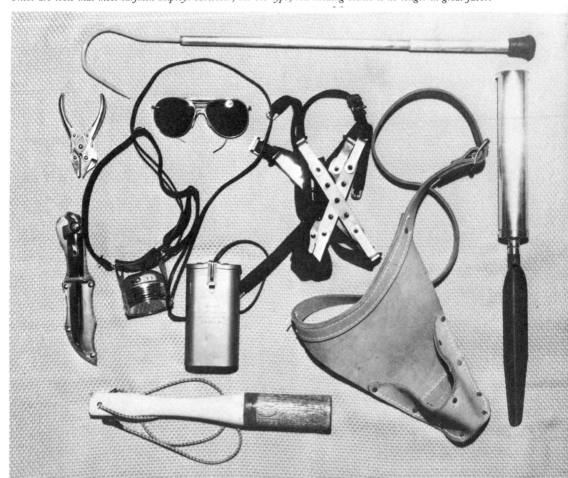

The matter continues to stir arm-waving argument. A harvest moon does not spook stripers: Indeed bragging catches are made on "moon tides" when it is possible to read a newspaper in the mid-watch. As mentioned before, lighthouses do not terrorize the legions, and bass are regularly taken under blazing dockside lights. Brothers and sisters who swim bottom baits in a staked-out area dote on glaring illumination provided by propane or gasoline-fueled pressure lanterns, and these appear to impose no handicap. To the contrary, folk who bet on the magic of the seaside footlights rightly declare that a steady glow concentrates the bait, and the bass follow the bait, and . . .

We cast our vote with those who prefer darkness, lamely preaching that stripers become accustomed to fixed lights, but are spooked by that which unaccountably appears and disappears. Simply detour around the well-illuminated camp sites of nighttime bait jockeys. If they are mannerly people, or if they simply avoid fisticuffs in the surf, they will refrain from invading *your* territory while you are humming a happy tune and throwing lures toward a blue-black horizon.

Striper Fisherman's Calendar

To GIVE THE EXACT DATES FOR THE ARRIVAL AND departure of striped bass along the coasts of the Atlantic and Gulf at any given geographical point is to flirt with disaster. However, unless there are extraordinary variations in such factors as weather, water temperatures, run-off, and bait supply, it is far easier to predict when the first fish will be taken in the spring than to prophesy when the bass will head south on their annual migrations.

Stripers that winter over in the deep holes of estuaries, rivers, or even offshore, normally may be taken throughout the cold season, yet they start to become active just about the same time as their migrating fellows arrive at a specific coastal point. Water temperature is the primary factor in triggering this type of activity, although variations in the amount of daylight as the vernal and autumnal equinoxes are approached may also have considerable effect on the fish's movements.

Almost everywhere throughout the striper's range, a few fish may be taken by angling die-hards in the dead of winter. In the calendar that follows, we have listed the times for what might be termed practical bass fishing—that is, fishing which may be enjoyed by an angler without ice freezing in the rod guides and with a reasonable chance of hooking a fish. "School bass" is used to designate fish from whatever the minimum length may be in the area up to 10 pounds; "large fish" are any specimens above that weight.

Record class "cows" may be taken almost anywhere. However, there are concentration spots where the chances of catching a new world record-beater are better than elsewhere. These areas include Cape Cod, and the islands lying south of it off the coast of Massachusetts; the Narrangansett, Newport, Jamestown, and Charlestown Beach sections of Rhode Island, with the Block Island waters thrown in for good measure; Montauk Point and the surrounding waters at the eastern tip of Long Island off New York; the Sandy Hook area off New Jersey, thence south to Seabright; much of Chesapeake Bay, with particular notice given to Virginia's Bay Bridge complex, the mouth of the Potomac River, and Brick House Bar off Matapeak; the Outer Banks of North Carolina. Check local laws, particulary in the Chesapeake, for the maximum weight and number of bass that may be retained. With the development of striper fishing going forward at full speed in the Gulf of Mexico, this also is potential record ground.

Although stripers weighing up to 65 pounds have been taken on the Pacific side by anglers—with a few specimens well above that weight noted by fisheries biologists—there seems to be no particular area where these large fish concentrate. The San Francisco Bay area in California and Coos Bay in Oregon are obvious potential grounds, but that says simply that records may be broken anywhere within the prime range of the species.

This appendix has been compiled from striper arrival and departure data gathered by the authors and by those who have contribted to *Salt Water Sportsman* for more than 40 years. Generally we have attempted to set down the approximate dates when bass appear in sufficient numbers to make fishing practical and enjoyable, and the dates when they cease to feed or depart for other waters. The calendar is meant to serve as a guide. As such, it will be found reasonably accurate—never infallible!

CANADA

Although anglers in Canada often curse striped bass because they hit flies intended for Atlantic salmon, increasing interest in the striper since the late 1960s has given rise to small groups of ardent bassers investigating in more detail waters where the fish may be found. Migratory patterns along many parts of the Canadian coast have yet to be firmly established, for the fish appear in a given area for several seasons in a row, then apparently vanish.

The Saint John River system in New Brunswick is one of the primary fishing grounds for both school and large specimens. In the Belle Isle River, commercial fishermen in the past seined bass through the ice in January, February, and March, but the angling season does not start until mid-June and runs through September. Further east, there are also bass in Chignecto Bay and the rivers flowing into it. Northward, most of the rivers famous for salmon also host stripers. The Miramichi and Tabisuntac are the best producers.

As previously noted, striped bass spawn throughout much of the Saint Lawrence River system in Quebec. Spring fishing is popular around Isle d'Orleans downstream from Quebec City for both school and large fish. Bass are taken all through the Saint Lawrence system during the summer, even though fishing pressure is comparatively slight.

In Nova Scotia, more anglers seek stripers than anywhere else in Canada. On the northern shore, Caribou Harbor near Pictou and waters thence eastward through Saint Georges Bay are best known for schoolies during the summer months. Sometimes there is a run of large bass for a few weeks during September near Arissig, but this is not necessarily an annual event.

Without question, the best striper fishing in this Province is in the Minas Basin area. At the head of Cobequid Bay is the Shubenacadie River, where bass spawn. From the last week of April through mid-June, school bass are the target, and from late June into October, large fish join them. Do not ask where stripers may be found, for the locals call them "tumblers" and catch them on earthworms!

The Annapolis River and Basin is another good spot for school bass, the best season being from mid-August to October. Because of the huge tides and roiled water, fishing is done primarily with bait, such as small herring, and the stripers ride in over the flats on the tide bore wave to feed upon creatures that the bore stirs up. From Yarmouth around to Mahone Bay at Chester, when the supply of schoolies is good coastwide, they are taken in many of the rivers, such as the Tusket, Clyde, Mersey, and Lehave. Catches are made in the autumn as far east as New Harbor and scattered fish are taken in the Cape Breton area, where effort to fish the species is minor. This last description also holds for Prince Edward Island.

MAINE

After striped bass returned in large numbers to New England waters in the late 1930s, it was some years before fishing fever for this species really infected Maine anglers. Undoubtedly summer tourists exposed locals to the merits of the fishery. Whatever the cause, there is now a growing group of striper addicts in Maine. The countless bays, rivers, and tidal streams along that coast provide excellent and diversified grounds.

Kittery–Cape Elizabeth: Light tackle fishing for school bass begins in late May as a general rule and continues through September. The Saco, Mousam, Pine Point, York, Kennebunk, and similar river systems yield stripers from "shorts" to fish in the five- to ten-pound class. Note that, when there is a dominant-year class of migrating small bass, these river systems often host fish all summer and in great numbers. These schoolies apparently forsake waters further south in New England if water temperatures are favorable to the north and east. Large stripers appear in late June and may be taken through September not only at the river mouths, but also along the beaches off York, Kennebunk, Ocean Park, and Old Orchard. This surf fishing is primarily a night operation. As is true along most of the southern Maine coast, there are also wintering bass, some of which are broken-striped.

Casco Bay–Rockland: Light tackle casting and trolling for school bass gets underway in the Androscoggin, New Meadow, Damariscotta, and Kennebec Rivers and their feeder streams about mid-June and continues through September. Large bass arrive during the first week of July and feed through September, the Damariscotta area being especially productive. Popham Beach is a hot spot for surf fishermen, but other outer beaches should not be ignored. A 64-pounder was taken in the vicinity of Boothbay in 1978, as an example of what may be available.

Penobscot Bay Eastward: School stripers are undoubtedly year-round residents in the Penobscot River system, but they seldom oblige anglers before June 15 or after late September. Good runs often appear in the Bangor Pool, where they are taken by anglers casting for Atlantic salmon. When water temperatures are warmer than usual, schoolies travel as far east as the Prettymarsh area of Mount Desert Island, but they are scarce east of that point. Large fish arrive in the coastal area during the first week in July and remain until late September. Prospecting along this part of the coast should pay off, for schoolies have been taken in lobster pots at many points where anglers are virtually unknown.

NEW HAMPSHIRE

In recent years, bass fishing has fallen off in the Granite State due, some claim, to pollution of the coastal river systems. School fish are predominant normally, but some large specimens have been landed in the past, primarily from waters at the mouth of the Piscataqua River or from the tide rips close to the abutments of the General Sullivan Bridge, which spans this waterway.

Hampton and Piscataqua River Systems: School stripers generally reach this area during the last week of May, most being taken by light tackle trolling. Hampton River Basin is a prime spot for these schoolies, which normally leave about the first week in October. Surf casting and trolling for large fish gets underway by June 15. These bass tend to move out before the end of September. The best spots for mid-summer angling are at the mouths of the Hampton and Piscataqua Rivers, the General Sullivan Bridge as noted above, Great and Little Bays, and Seabrook Beach.

MASSACHUSETTS

Massachusetts is the northernmost of the great Atlantic Coast striper fishing grounds. By location and tradition, its waters offer some of the best surf, offshore, and light tackle angling on the East Coast, for it is here that many migrants spend the summer. The season runs from approximately

May 1 into late November, with school fish predominating in spring and fall. Large stripers appear in small numbers by mid-May, but concentrations are most likely to be present from June 1 to October 1 along the mainland coast, and from June 1 to November 15 around Nantucket, Martha's Vineyard, and the Elizabeth Islands chain, which includes the famous grounds off Cuttyhunk.

Nantucket–Martha's Vineyard–Cuttyhunk: These are the famous islands, but they are only part of a chain that includes more than a half-dozen—and a great deal of good bass water, both surf and offshore. Squidding for school stripers begins on the Vineyard about May 1 and continues through November. Note, however, that a few wintering fish are caught annually as early as the first week in March, primarily from the openings of the many tidal ponds. Large bass appear by June 1, but the best fishing is reserved for late fall.

The Cuttyhunk timetable is similar, but anglers rarely go after school bass around that island, which is noted for its monsters. Trolling and casting on the offshore rips is a Cuttyhunk specialty. Bass boats from this island, from neighboring Martha's Vineyard, and from the mainland ports of New Bedford and Westport, go into action about the first of June. Thereafter, until almost mid-November, very large bass are taken from the offshore rips and reefs, often at night. There is surf fishing from the shores of all the Elizabeth Island chain, but because the islands for the most part are privately owned, visiting anglers must stick to their boats.

Nantucket spring fishing also gets underway during the first week of May with the peak of the season from June to November. The pattern is similar to that of Martha's Vineyard and Cuttyhunk. However, when bluefish are plentiful around Nantucket itself, bass tend to move out into the many rips and channels found around the neighboring islands of Tuckernuck and Muskeget, particularly in the late summer and early fall.

Cape Cod: Light tackle surf casting and trolling for school fish gets underway about May 1 and continues through November, although a few wintering fish are taken prior to May. First catches are usually made in the Buzzards Bay–Falmouth–Cotuit areas during the first week of May. The Weweantic River, in the town of Wareham, is an early producer of schoolies. The Taunton and Westport Rivers also yield early school bass, while Succonnessett Beach, Wianno, and New Harbor (east of Falmouth), Wings Neck, Bird Island, and the Buzzards Bay sand spit along the Cape Cod Canal are equally productive.

School bass and occasional large fish are taken from all Cape Cod river systems and beaches by May 15, but not in great numbers. At the same time, trollers in Massachusetts Bay on the north side of the Cape begin to take fair catches of both school and large bass. Fishing also gets underway at this time in the Cape Cod Canal.

Surf casting, trolling, and light tackle fishing for bass of all sizes is well underway on the Cape Cod tidal rivers, beaches, and offshore waters by the third week in May. The stretch of beach from Provincetown to Monomoy, much of which is now a National Seashore, is known as the Outer Cape and provides prime surf fishing. The Billingsgate area, off Wellfleet, is favored by trollers, but also pleases plug casters when bass are rushing bait on the surface.

The peak of the Cape Cod season begins about the first of June and continues through October. Big fish are present in greatest numbers between June 1 and September 15. These large bass normally are concentrated in the following locations: the Cape Cod Canal; Billingsgate; Race Point at Provincetown; Peaked Hill Bars and the Meadows in North Truro, thence southward along the beach to Nauset Inlet at Orleans; Morris and Monomoy Islands at Chatham. Note also that Pleasant Bay on the inside of the barrier beach yields both school and large bass.

South Shore: Light tackle fishing and trolling for school bass in the river systems of the South Shore begins about the third week of May and continues through early October. The North River, at Scituate, is the most important producer, but all streams in the vicinity hold considerable numbers of bass.

Surf casting, trolling, and light tackle fishing for school bass in the bays and off the beaches gets underway by May 15. Sagamore Beach, Plymouth, and Duxbury Bays, Humarock, the area at the mouth of the North River, Hull, and Boston Harbor itself—which geographically may not be considered part of the South Shore—all yield fish. Large bass appear about mid-June in these areas and move out in early November.

North Shore Light tackle trolling and casting for school bass begins by the third week of May and continues through early October. River systems, such as those of the Annisquam, Parker, and Merrimack, yield the first schoolies and some of these are stripers that have wintered over. Large bass appear around mid-June and remain through early October.

Although both school and large bass are taken along the entire North Shore, from Boston Harbor north through Nahant, Marblehead, and Rockport, the Plum Island area is favored by many anglers. Here, from June 15 through early October, big bass are taken by surf casters on the beach and by trollers working just off the Plum Island jetties. In summertime night fishing is especially productive.

RHODE ISLAND

Rhode Island is another of the great striper fishing states on the Atlantic seaboard. Its waters have yielded many of the world's largest rod-and-reel bass, plus great catches of school fish. Generally the season is spring and fall, although stripers are present from April to December and some fish winter over in Rhode Island waters. Unlike Massachusetts, Rhode Island's large bass are most plentiful during October and November.

Watch Hill to Weekapaug: School stripers become active in the surf and river systems in late April, from about the 20th of the month, and some remain there until late November. Surf casting, trolling, and light tackle fishing is best in spring and fall, although they may be profitable throughout the year. Large bass arrive about May 15, but angling is sporadic until October, when it usually breaks wide open. Offshore and close inshore trollers are usually successful.

Quonochontaug to Point Judith: Here again, school bass begin to feed in the surf, river systems, and inlets by late April and remain through November. Quonochontaug, Charlestown Beach and Breachway, Matunuck Beach, and Point Judith are hot spots. Spring fishing for schoolies is excellent. Large bass arrive about May 15, but the sport is not at its peak until October and November. At that time, Charlestown Beach and the Breachway yield some of the largest stripers of the season.

Narragansett Bay: Light tackle casting and trolling for school bass in the river systems and the bay itself begins about May 1. As noted, some stripers remain in this area the year around, but the season is generally conceded to be May through November. Occasionally large bass are taken inside Narragansett Bay, but small fish are more likely there.

Trophy fish are usually concentrated at the mouth of the bay. Such famous locations as Beavertail, Brenton Point, Newport, and Sakonnet Point have yielded huge bass, several of which have been within a few pounds of the world record. Much of the fishing here is done from small boats, with anglers either casting into the surf or trolling just off the rocks.

Surf casting, boat casting, trolling, and light tackle fishing for both school and large bass in the lower bay area starts around mid-June and continues through November. For large bass, the peak of the season comes during October and November.

Block Island: Block Island can provide either feast or famine striper fishing. Water temperature apparently is the key. When the ocean is abnormally cold, bass may by-pass the area on their migrations, particularly during the spring. In a normal year, school fish move in after mid-April and remain through November. Their larger relatives arrive a month later and also stay until the late fall. Both surf and offshore fishing is good from June 1 to November 15, with the best time normally from mid-October to mid-November.

CONNECTICUT

Because of its location on the northwest shore of the Long Island Sound, Connecticut misses the great migrating runs of large bass, but it does enjoy some excellent school striper fishing from stocks from both the Hudson River and Chesapeake Bay. Occasional big fish are taken, but the Nutmeg State angler rarely runs into pods of bass in the 30- to 50-pound class. A great deal of fishing is done from small boats, either in the river systems or along the coasts of the offshore islands. Surf and light tackle casting also accounts for many stripers, predominantly of the school variety.

The state has a long and action-packed season. Bass are present in many rivers throughout the year. The Thames at Norwich and New London begins to produce fish early in March, or even late in February. The Niantic, a few miles south, also yields bass from late March to November. Cold-weather angling is, however, extremely spotty and many of the river systems go into a slump during the mid-summer season.

Greenwich–Cos Cob: Light tackle casting and trolling begins in earnest after April 15 and bass arrive on the outside reefs during the first week of May. This entire area is a hot spot for school bass. Occasional large fish are taken after June 1. The season runs through November and is especially kind to light tackle buffs. One word of warning: Check local laws, for in some of the estuarine waters, a fresh water fishing license is required.

Norwalk–Darien: School stripers begin to feed in the river systems by April 15, but coastal angling does not get underway before the first week in May. Surf, light tackle casting, and trolling are good at the river mouths and around the Fish Islands, off Darien and around the Norwalk Islands from May 15 through November. School bass are most numerous, but there are a few large fish also.

Southport to Housatonic River: School stripers move into the river systems by April 15. Light tackle trolling and casting are most productive at the river mouths and on the beaches close to them. Large bass appear about mid-May and remain through November, but they are nowhere very abundant.

New Haven to Connecticut River: The seasons for school and large bass are the same as for the Southport–Housatonic area listed above. Small stripers are taken in the lower reaches of the Connecticut River at about the same time that the shad run starts in late April. The river mouth at Saybrook Point and adjacent coastal areas are favored.

Niantic–New London: School stripers, probably resident, begin to hit light tackle lures and bait in the river systems by late March. Prior to that time, good catches of Thames River bass are sometimes made by fishing the deep holes. Both the Thames and Niantic provide fair to good early-season angling for schoolies, with bass moving towards the Sound as the waters warm up. Spring and fall offer the best sport and normally there is a cessation of activity in mid-summer.

School bass and occasional large ones arrive in this area by May 15. Surf casting, trolling, and all light tackle fishing is fair to good at the river mouths, on the beaches, and along the coast of Fishers Island lying off New London. As elsewhere in the state, catches are made through November.

Mystic–Stonington: School stripers normally begin to hit after mid-April and occasional large bass move into this area by May 15; all remain in the general area until late November. Trollers and casters concentrate on Fishers Island Sound, at Groton Long Point, Mason Island, Stonington, and Napatree Point.

NEW YORK

In addition to supplying some of the best striped bass fishing on the Atlantic Coast, New York also holds the key to striper abundance in Long Island Sound and the Sandy Hook, New Jersey, area. The Hudson River, although it is seriously polluted, is a spawning ground of considerable importance and an area in which bass are year-round residents.

School stripers supply most of the action in Long Island Sound and in the upper and lower bays of New York, but the South Shore of Long Island is big fish water. Montauk, out on the island's tip, ranks as one of the great striper fishing locations of the world. Boat casting and trolling close to shore is most profitable from a big fish standpoint, yet surf casting also produces good catches of school and large bass.

Hudson River: Although a few anglers take stripers throughout the year from the waters of the Hudson, practical light tackle casting and trolling normally begins about April 1. For school fish in particular, April and early May are prime times, and a few large bass are taken all the way up the river as far as Albany. The run tapers off during the summer, but the fish are back again in the fall. Native stocks, particularly near the mouth of the Hudson, are augmented by migrators from southern waters during the seasonal cycles.

New York Bight: The waters at the mouth of the Hudson annually produce good hauls of school stripers and occasional large fish. The first bass normally are taken in mid-April and the season continues through early December. In recent years, some of the heavily traveled waterways, such as the East River and waters around Governor's Island, have yielded bass of all sizes, particularly during the autumn months.

West End–Long Island South: Metropolitan area anglers often begin their bassing season in this area. Light tackle casting and trolling for school stripers gets underway about April 15 and continues through November with, normally, a slack period during mid-summer. Flushing, Little Neck and Manhasset Bays, Glen Cove, New Rochelle, and Mamaroneck all supply good catches of schoolies. Large bass in limited quantities arrive by May 1 and remain through November.

North Shore–Long Island: Light tackle casting and trolling is practiced along the entire North Shore from mid-April through November. School bass are the most numerous with occasional large fish taken. From Lloyd Harbor to Orient Point is the usual fishing ground, but schoolies often run around into Gardiner's Bay and can be taken off Shelter Island with a few bass joining the weakfish in Peconic Bay.

Jamaica Bay and the Rockaways: School bass arrive late in April and the first fishing is primarily light tackle trolling and casting. Surf fishing in this area starts during the first week in May and continues through November. However, most of the shore angling is light tackle work at inlets and from, or near, bridge structures. Large bass are rare.

South Shore–Long Island: New York's finest surf casting beaches are located on the South Shore from Rockaway Point to Montauk. Light tackle trolling and casting for school bass gets underway by May 1 and continues through November. Large stripers reach the area by May 15 and are available during the remainder of the season. Progressing from west to east, the favored locations are Atlantic Beach, Long Beach and Fire Island, Fire Island Inlet, Great South Bay, Shinnecock Inlet, and Montauk. The last named is one of the great striped bass fishing areas of the coast, with surf casting and trolling dividing the honors. Here, as at Cuttyhunk, specialized bass boats are used close in to the rock-studded surf.

NEW JERSEY

New Jersey is another of the great Atlantic Coast bass fishing states, and the only one able to boast that its stripers are the progenitors of the entire Pacific fishery. Bass taken from the Navesink and Shrewsbury Rivers during the latter part of the nineteenth century were planted at Carquinez Straits and Suisan Bay in California.

Generally school stripers are most abundant from Delaware Bay north to Sandy Hook, but there is no scarcity of large bass. Indeed, the tide rips off the Hook qualify that area as one of the most important coastal concentrations for record-class stripers. Boat fishing during the peak of the season (June through early November) accounts for many bass in the 40- to 50-pound class, and there normally are a few weighing better than the much-sought-after half-hundred mark.

North Shore–Delaware Bay: Light tackle casting and trolling for school bass can start in late March. Many of these fish may well be from local stocks, since fish are taken through December and even later. Schoolies predominate, as they do in the Cape May section, but Bay fish remain available throughout the summer while Cape May bassing is basically a spring and autumn operation.

Atlantic City Area: School stripers are resident and are taken from the sod banks and from small craft in the vast tracts of marshland west of Atlantic City itself. Practical fishing generally is limited to the April–December period. Light tackle casting and trolling in the river systems and inlets is most productive, while surfing at the inlets and jetties is fair to good. Great Egg Harbor Bay and River, Mullica River, Brigantine and Absecon Inlets are favorite spots. Spring and fall are the best fishing periods.

Barnegat to Bayhead: Barnegat Bay, its river systems and inlets, all produce school bass from April 1 through December, but spring and fall fishing are best, with the emphasis on fall. As is true of Little Egg Harbor and Great Bay to the south, light tackle is the general rule in the waters behind the barrier beaches. On the ocean side, good surf fishing from the beaches and jetties begins around the first of May and continues through the summer months, reaching a peak in the fall. Toms River is the central point in the inland waterway and provides good fishing for schoolies.

Island Beach and Long Beach Island, north and south respectively of Barnegat Inlet, yield both school bass and some large ones. Here squidding often starts as early as mid-March for the small fish, slacks off in the summer, then improves again in September, October, and early November for larger fish.

Point Pleasant: Aside from the initial run of school bass, which often hits this area in late March, light tackle fishing for schoolies from the Chesapeake begins about May 1 and continues through early December. The Manasquan River and Canal are favored locations for night fishermen. Point Pleasant Beach and Sea Girt produce bass for the surfman and jetty jockey.

Sea Girt to Long Branch: Aside from Shark River and Shark River Inlet, this stretch of New Jersey beach is squidding territory. School bass are in the surf from May 1 through December, but the best fishing is in spring and fall. Light tackle fishing in the river systems gets underway by April 1 and continues through early December.

Belmar to Sea Bright: Light tackle casting and trolling for school bass and occasional large fish, perhaps wintering-over specimens, gets underway in the Shrewsbury and Navesink Rivers as early as April 1 and continues through November. Although the Shrewsbury Rocks area off Monmouth Beach is best known for bluefish, it also yields good catches of stripers. Long Branch Beach, Monmouth Beach, and the coast north to Highlands is productive in spring and fall, with sporadic catches in mid-summer. A 64-pounder was caught in late June of 1971 off Sea Bright, which indicates that some of those sporadic catches are worth seeking!

Sandy Hook: As previously noted, this is one of New Jersey's hot spots for huge bass. Park lands at the Hook itself produce well for surf fishermen, and trolling in the rips of the area gets results for boatmen. Schoolies arrive in this area in late April, but big fish rarely show until late in May. By mid-

November, most of the stripers have left the area.

Lower Bay and Raritan River: Light tackle casting and trolling for school bass begins in the river systems about April 1 and continues through early December. Occasional big fish are taken, but it is primarily a feeding grounds for schoolies. From May 1 through November, school and large bass are taken by trollers working the Bay shore from the Raritan River to Union Beach.

DELAWARE

Waters of this state have long been considered prime spawning grounds for striped bass, but production was reduced greatly over a long period of years by major pollution in the Delaware River and Bay. Conditions have been improving steadily and, before long, stripers may well be re-established in sufficient numbers to rival the Hudson River in New York and some of the river systems in Chesapeake Bay.

Delaware Bay: Some bass are taken throughout the year, but the sport fishing season usually begins between March 15 and March 30 for all practical purposes. It continues through early December on both resident and migratory fish. School and large stripers are taken by surf fishing and light tackle casting near the Bay entrance in the vicinity of Lewes and northwestward to Slaughter Beach. Small boat trolling and casting is becoming more and more popular in this area and well up into the Delaware River.

Rehoboth and Indian River Bays: Light tackle casting and small boat trolling is preferred in these localities and fishing dates are similar to those in Delaware Bay itself. Schoolies predominate, but some large bass are taken from the ocean side beaches, particularly in the autumn.

Indian River Inlet: By all accounts, this is Delaware's most popular striper fishing location. Casting from the beach for school bass and the occasional large specimen gets underway toward the end of March and continues throughout December. Small boat operators also do well. Even during the mid-winter months, a few bass are taken by hardy anglers. South of the Inlet itself, along Bethany Beach, there is some surf fishing, but it is a hit-or-miss proposition, for the stripers apparently do not linger long in their travels.

MARYLAND AND THE
DISTRICT OF COLUMBIA

The keeping of large striped bass in Maryland waters was prohibited for many years by law, which resulted in the lack of development of a big bass fishery. Now, however, except during the spawning season from March through May, anglers may keep one striper over 15 pounds per day. However, most anglers still concentrate on schoolies.

No attempt has been made in what follows to list every inlet, cove, or feeder stream that flows into Chesapeake Bay, for bass at times may be found almost anywhere and fishing is a year-round game. For practical purposes, the sport fishery may be set from mid-March to December.

Fenwick and Assateague Islands: Along this outer beach, surf fishing can be productive during the spring migrations in April and the fall migrations in November. At other times, bass are scarce indeed. Boat fishermen can connect at the same seasons further offshore at such spots as Fox Hill Levels and South Pond. Around Ocean City Inlet, stripers may be taken through much of the season except in the heat of summer. Small boat fishermen also do well inside the Inlet in the Isle of Wight Bay.

Susquehanna, Elk, and Sassafras Rivers: Working down the Chesapeake from north to south, boat fishermen take stripers from the rivers themselves and from areas further offshore, such as the Susquehanna Flats, with peak fishing from April to mid-June. Shore casters also pick up fish throughout the year in the Turkey Point area. Note that, in times of drought, stripers tend to move further south in the Bay and foresake this area to a large degree.

Gunpowder Neck–Worton Point Area: Trolling and some light tackle fishing produces stripers in this area; the best fishing is from mid-August to November 1. The west side of the Bay around Aberdeen Proving Grounds is largely restricted. Phoenix Shoal off Worton Creek is a local hot spot.

Pooles Island–Rock Hall Area: South of Pooles Island is a whole series of shoals, such as the Lumps, Tea Table, Gales Lumps, and Mitchells Bluff Bar, that provide excellent trolling as well as light tackle casting for bass. April through May and October through November are the peak seasons. On the western shore, fishing in the Patapsco River itself is poor, but Man O' War and Bodkin Point Shoals outside the river mouth produce well. Windmill Point at Rock Hall hosts some bass all year.

Gibson Island to Bloody Point: This area includes a vast amount of good striped bass water on both sides of the Bay. The Magothy River and Mountain Point Bar near Gibson Island, for example, produce best from April through June and again in September and October; across the Bay, the Chester River yields bass all through the year and they run well above Chestertown. Across the whole Bay is the Annapolis Bridge, which is a prime man-made bassing area for trolling, boat casting, drifting, and jigging. Charter and private boats cover this section on such grounds as Brick House Bar, Gum Thicket, Wild Grounds, and The Hole west of Bloody Point, which itself is a spot where large fish are taken from late November to February.

Kent Island divides the Chesapeake at this point into the Chester River to the north and Eastern Bay, with its countless tributaries, to the south. Peak seasons in the many small bays vary greatly and consultation with local watermen and tackle shop operators is recommended.

Deal to Taylors Island: In this area, the western shoreline is relatively unbroken, but the eastern is a maze of creeks, islets, marshes, and flats in the Choptank River estuary. Holland Point Bar and Winter Gooses are the primary trolling grounds on the western side whose peaks are in spring and late fall. As is true in the Chester River area, the grounds in the Choptank estuary vary greatly during the seasons and they run up the river itself as far as Dover Bridge. In general, large bass are taken in the spring and late fall while schoolies may be caught both then and through the summer.

Cove Point to Smith Point: On the western shore, striper fishing follows the pattern that best catches for both school and large bass are made in spring and fall, with the mouths of the Patuxent and Potomac Rivers as prime areas. As noted elsewhere, some very big fish congregate around the Potomac in January and February. Across the Bay, bass fishing is a year-round activity with school fish predominating during the summer months. Here again the maze of creeks, channels, and islands around the Honga River, Fishing Bay, and Tangier Sound provide good fishing mainly for trollers and boat casters, for many of the shore areas are difficult to reach by road. Southwest of the Hooper Islands is a favored trolling area for charter and private boats. Further south, the Southwest Middle Grounds are most productive in early autumn.

VIRGINIA

As in Maryland, catches of large striped bass were prohibited for many years in Virginian waters, so the school bass fishery predominated. The law governing retention of trophy fish now is similar to that of Maryland, with the result that larger bass are taken regularly, particularly in the Bay Bridge–Tunnel area.

Tangier Island to Cape Charles: As is true of much of Chesapeake Bay, rivers, creeks and inlets on both the western and eastern shores produce both school and large bass. Fall fishing is best in mid-Bay, west of the Tangier Sound entrance, while spots such as Cut Channel to the south produce school bass through much of the year. The Rappahannock River and estuary, waters around Gwynn Island and New Point Comfort, Mobjack Bay, and the York River are good for school fish in spring and fall. Across the bay, the waters are better-known for channel bass than stripers, but many of the latter are also to be found in such spots as Chesonnessex, which is favored from May through September.

Hampton and Bridge–Tunnel Area: Back River and the Willoughby Bank section are the best bets for bass, particularly during the spring runs. However, as noted, the Bridge–Tunnel complex predominates as a fishing spot for both school and large bass in this part of the lower Bay. Trolling, drifting, and casting, anglers can take fish throughout the year, with the heaviest bass likely from mid-November through December. In addition, boat fishing south of Fisherman Island and north and east of Fort Story is good in spring and fall.

Outer Coast: North of Myrtle Island, striper fishing is poor, but from that point south, there is normally an excellent run of fish, many of them large, in the fall. November is the favored month for trollers. Along the entire Virginia Beach section, both inshore and offshore, the autumn is again the best time, although school fish also appear close to shore from April through June. This pattern holds true all the way to the North Carolina line.

NORTH CAROLINA

For many years, large striped bass off the North Carolina beaches frustrated anglers, but more and more are being taken today by anglers surf casting with both lures and natural bait. The sounds and inlets produce both large and small bass.

Virginia Line to Oregon Inlet: Surf fishing for large bass is best from September through November along this entire stretch of beach. Schoolies are more abundant during the April–June period. A couple of miles offshore from the state line to Corolla, trollers connect with big bass well into December.

Pea Island to Cape Fear: Striped bass concentrate in the surf from Pea Island down to Hatteras Inlet during December and January, but they normally are fussy feeders. For the most part, these are very large fish. At times, they may move offshore to the western edge of the Gulf Stream. They are also taken in trolling east of Cape Fear, but west of that point they are rare.

Currituck, Pamlico, and Albemarle Sounds: Stripers, both school and large bass, are found in all the river systems draining into these sounds. The largest fish on record—125 pounds—was netted in April, 1891, off Edenton at the mouth of the Chowan River. Many bass travel far upstream, more than 100 miles from salt water, and may never see the ocean again during their entire life cycle.

Best fishing both in the river systems and the sounds is from late March to June and again from mid-September to mid-December. The favored spots are off Nells Creek in Currituck Sound in late fall; the North River mouth and Durant Island areas in Albemarle, spring and fall; Roanoke and Croatan Sound Bridges, late fall; Croatan Sound itself, primarily for school fish, from March through May and again in November and December; the major tributaries to Pamlico Sound during the same general seasons, some fish being taken during the summer months.

SOUTH CAROLINA

Most of the striped bass fishing in South Carolina is for riverine fish that stick to fresh or brackish water. The best seasons for bassing throughout the state are from late March to late June, then again from September through November, although some fish are taken throughout the year from deep holes. Casting and slow trolling are the favored methods of fishing.

Moving from north to south, the best producing areas are Waccamaw River and Winyah Bay; North and South Santee Rivers, with the impoundments of Lakes Moultrie and Marion offering landlocked striper fishing; Wando River; Cooper and Ashley Rivers; North and South Edisto Rivers; tributaries to Saint Helena Sound and to Port Royal Sound; the Savannah River on the Georgia border.

GEORGIA

Striped bass fishing in Georgia is very similar to that in South Carolina, although the species has not become popular among Georgia anglers. Rivers that are known to produce fish include, in addition to the Savannah, the Ogeechee, Ohoopee, Altamaha, Satilla, and Saint Mary's on the Florida border. Bass in some of these rivers are found well over 100 miles above the river mouths.

In the old Flint River, which runs into the Spring River and thence into Florida's Apalachicola and the Gulf of Mexico, there is a spring run of both school and large bass, plus a fall run of the same fish. Stripers weighing up to 60 pounds have been taken by trotline in the Devil's Den area, near Bainbridge. Anglers also take fish in this area by casting and trolling.

Bass have become landlocked behind the Woodruff Dam, as was the case in Lakes Marion and Moultrie in South Carolina, and there is now a fishery there for the species.

FLORIDA

Florida's striped bass fishing is limited, particularly on the Atlantic side, but there are definite resident river populations. As is true of other southern states, stripers are found far upriver from salt water. For anglers, the peak seasons are April and May, then again in September and October, although some bass are taken throughout the year.

Saint Mary's River to Saint Johns: Bass are taken in the river systems west of Fernandina Beach and Amelia Island, notably in the Saint Mary's on the Georgia border and in the Nassau. The Saint Johns River, however, is the best known on Florida's Atlantic coast. There are some large bass, but catches are predominantly schoolies. For practical fishing, this must be considered the southern limit for bass.

Northwest Coast: From the Ochlockonee River westward to the Perdido River on the Alabama border is the range for striped bass along Florida's Gulf coast. Besides these two rivers, the best known are the Chipola, Apalachicola, Yellow, Blackwater, and Escambia. Native stocks in many cases have been augmented by stocking programs over a long period of years. Striped bass play second fiddle to many other species in this area. They run extraordinary distances up the river systems. School fish are the most plentiful and large bass rarely top 30 pounds. Near the Gulf itself, night trolling is the most productive method of bass fishing in spring and fall.

ALABAMA

Alabama's comparatively short coastline produces some school and large striped bass, but basically the fishing is in the river system, where fish appear at times hundreds of miles from salt water. The peak seasons are from mid-April all through May, then again in November and December.

Mobile Bay Area: Night plug casting, drifting, and some trolling are the usual methods employed in this area. Native stocks have been augmented by some stocking, as is true along much of the Gulf Coast.

Alabama River Systems: Amazing runs of stripers, some of them weighing up to 50 pounds, travel better than 300 miles through the Alabama River system, with most catches occurring in the Coosa and Tallapoosa. The best season is from late April to mid-June, but some are taken throughout the year. Favored locations are below the falls at Wetumpka on the Coosa, and a couple of miles below Tallahassee near a similar falls on the Tallapoosa. There is, in addition, some fishing as far upstream as Montgomery. Plug casting and still fishing with bait are the most common angling methods.

MISSISSIPPI

Striped bass fishing here is very similar to that found in Alabama. Both school and large bass are found in all the river systems from the Pascagoula River west to the Tangipahoa. They are also taken far up the Mississippi River itself. As is true elsewhere along the Gulf, stocking has increased the supply, but the fishing is basically done in the rivers rather than in salt water.

Mississippi River Systems: Besides the rivers mentioned above, the best known areas are in the Jourdan, Wolf, and Tchouticabouffa Rivers. Peak fishing for both school and large bass is from April through May, with a fall run from late October through mid-December. Some fish are taken throughout the year. Casting from the river banks, from small craft, and still fishing with bait are the usual methods.

LOUISIANA

Native striped bass evidently were present for years in all the river systems of Louisiana, but the main supply today is the result of stocking. Since 1965, when these programs were initiated, the striper fishery has been growing rapidly not only in the river systems, but also in the estuaries and into the Gulf itself. Undoubtedly this expansion will continue, so exploration should pay off for anglers willing to experiment.

Louisiana Coast: Because of the huge complex of islets, marshes, and creeks in the delta area of Louisiana, it is difficult to pinpoint concentrations of stripers. However, native bass originally were found in the Tchefuncta and Tickfauw Rivers and are still there. Since stocking was started on a fairly large scale, the best waters are at the mouth of the Mississippi River, in Barataria Bay, and in the Calcasieu, Mermentau, and Sabine Rivers. This is basically a small boat fishery for casters, trollers, and still fishermen. Peak seasons are from late March to June and October and November for both school and large bass. Night fishing pays off for the latter.

TEXAS

It is doubtful that there ever was a population of striped bass of any magnitude in Texas waters. Because of a stocking program, today there is a viable fishery in the San Antonio Bay area with school fish predominating. The peak seasons are similar to those of Louisiana. The finest sport is found where bass have been released into a number of landlocked fresh water lakes.

CALIFORNIA

Striped bass are not native Californians, having been introduced from the Atlantic seaboard first in 1879, later in 1881. For the record, that initial stocking of 132 bass from New Jersey's Navesink River went into the Carquinez Straits near Pittsburg. More recent immigrants from the Atlantic, released in Southern California during the mid-1970s, originated in South Carolina's Santee–Cooper impoundments.

In the San Francisco Bay area, a total of 435 stripers stocked in 1879 and 1881 prospered and, by the end of the century, produced a remarkably profitable sport and commercial fishery. The state no longer permits sale, although there is considerable black market activity.

Far southward in the general vicinity of San Diego, the somewhat promising survival of fish released during the mid to late 1970s intrigues marine biologists and on-site anglers. It is, however, currently doubtful that this effort will result in anything other than a put-and-take fishery, since drastic fluctuations of fresh water levels may adversely effect natural spawning.

Well-established and viable stocks of striped bass remain limited to Central California's San Francisco Bay area north to Oregon. San Francisco, its river and delta spawning grounds, the bay itself—together with outside beaches adjacent to the Golden Gate—comprise the striper mecca of the West. While no angler of this seaboard has yet seriously challenged the IGFA all-tackle mark, marine biologists have documented bass weighing better than 80 pounds. Therefore, a new record rod-and-reel catch is within the realm of possibility.

Southern California: Stripers released in San Diego Bay, in the San Diego River Flood Control Channel, and at Agua Hedionda Lagoon somewhat up-coast has resulted in the promising survival of a likely put-and-take stocking. During the 1981 season anglers accounted for relatively small numbers of bass ranging from three to five pounds on average, up to approximately ten pounds. February and March appear to be the peak fishing months and most of the fish are caught on ghost shrimp bait.

Martin's Beach: Seven miles south of Half Moon Bay, Martin's Beach witnesses an annual summer run of bass ranging from school size up to a hoped-for average of 20-pounders and scattered fish that will pull the scales to 30 pounds or somewhat better. This is a catch-as-catch-can operation, since stripers appear to visit the area only when surf smelt are spawning in the summer months.

San Francisco: Seasonal angling can be excellent in the Bay itself, on adjacent beaches to the north and south, in spawning areas such as the Sacramento San Joaquin River Delta and river systems including the Sacramento, San Joaquin, Yuba, Feather, and American. Bottom baits score best in the brackish, often muddy delta areas during the months March, April, and May.

Bay action peaks from late April through summer and early fall, often continuing well into November, although practically all stripers are out of salt water by December. Boatmen enjoy a lion's share of the San Francisco Bay action.

Fine surf fishing, south of the Golden Gate and north to Point Bonita, is at peak about mid-July, although there is a build-up starting in late June and often continuing through August. Favored strands are Baker's Beach, Land's Inn, Ocean Beach, Fleishhacker's Beach, Thornton Beach, Mussel Rock, Pacifica Beach, Linda Mar Beach—after which one skips several miles of steep cliffs south to Pillar Point Harbor, Francis Beach, and Martin's. Rarely are bass taken south of the Salinas River. Average linesides weigh between 15 and 20 pounds and some go 30 or better. Central California's surf is rough and anglers almost always suffer the attention of onshore winds as they cast whole or cut sardines, anchovies, mackerel, squid, and sea worms, plus metal jigs and plugs. Night fishing is permitted, but few sportsmen work the grounds between sunset and dawn.

There are scattered numbers of striped bass in Tomales Bay and at the mouth of the Russian River from late spring through summer and fall. Angling is considered spotty in the two areas and the best catches are made by local specialists.

OREGON

Coos Bay: Excellent boat fishing occurs during summer and fall, with peak sport from June through September and early October. Surf casting is limited, although some good catches are made from shore. Bass range from schoolies up to a good number of middleweights and a few real trophies. Natural baits, either cut or whole, get big play. Plugs, spoons, metal jigs, and flies do well.

Umpqua River: From tidewater to fresh, stripers are taken from shore and boat from mid-May through September and early October. Fish are school-sized, up to 20 and 30 pounds, with a scattering of heavyweights to add spice. Again, natural baits are favored, but artificial lures of all types hit the jackpot on night and day sorties.

North of Oregon's Coos Bay and Umpqua River there is no striped bass fishery worthy of note. Only occasional strays are taken from the coastal rivers of the State of Washington.

Index

Note: References to illustrations are indicated by italics.